THE ART OF SERENITY

◆

*The Path to a Joyful Life
in the Best and Worst of Times*

T. BYRAM KARASU, M.D.

SIMON & SCHUSTER

NEW YORK LONDON TORONTO SYDNEY SINGAPORE

SIMON & SCHUSTER
Rockefeller Center
1230 Avenue of the Americas
New York, NY 10020

For information regarding special discounts for bulk purchases,
please contact Simon & Schuster Special Sales at 1-800-456-6798
or business@simonandschuster.com

Manufactured in the United States of America

10   9   8   7   6   5   4   3   2

Library of Congress Cataloging-in-Publication Data
Karasu, Toksoz B.
    The art of serenity : the path to a joyful life in the best and worst
        of times / T. Byram Karasu.
        p.   cm.
    Includes bibliographical references.
1. Spiritual life. 2. Self-actualization (Psychology)—Religious aspects.
I. Title.
BL624 .K3356   2003
291.4—dc21   2002030493

ISBN 0-7432-2831-6

Permissions appear on page 241.

ACKNOWLEDGMENTS

*What am I myself? What have I done? I have col-
lected and used everything that I have heard and
observed. My work has been nourished by thousands
of diverse individuals—ignorant and sage, genius and
fool, infant and elderly. They all offer me their abili-
ties and their way of being. Often I have reaped the
harvest that others have sown. My work is that of a
collective being, and it carries the name of Goethe.*

—Goethe[*]

The content of this book reflects our collective knowledge
and wisdom. I made every effort to identify the original
authors in every statement in the text. But it is not easy to
give credit to their influence, especially when some of their
sayings have become a matter of common parlance; others I
remember having read or heard somewhere, but I couldn't
place them. Though I cannot acknowledge all of my literary
debts, I am consoled by Suzanne Langer that this isn't so
unusual. She says: "Inevitably, the philosophical ideas of
every thinker stem from all he has read as well as all he has
heard and seen, and if consequently little of his material is
really original, that only lends his doctrines the continuity of

[*]From original conversation with Swiss scientist Frederic Soret, February 17,
1832. Frederic Soret: *Zehn Jahre Bei Goethe* (*Ten Years with Goethe*), ed.
Heinrich Hubert Houben (Leipzig: F. A. Brockhaus, 1929), p. 630.

an old intellectual heritage."* Please consider, therefore, what is said here as an amalgam of ideas by some or all wise men and women over the centuries.

More specifically, I owe the realization of this book to a number of extraordinary people: I am especially thankful to my exceptionally gifted editor, Sydny Miner, whose vision, encouragement, and confidence were invaluable. She patiently and graciously guided every step of the publication process with impeccable skills and wisdom. I am also thankful to Victoria Meyer and Aileen Boyle for their enthusiastic reception, Martha Schwartz for her genteel shepherding, Susan Brown for her scrupulous copyediting, and all other staff of Simon & Schuster associated with the project. I want to express my appreciation to my agent/lawyer Ronald Konecky, for his sage advice and generous efforts on my behalf.

I am most indebted to Betty Meltzer for her literary assistance, with enduring intellectual interest, engagement, dedication, and unsurpassed competence. I am grateful to Hilda Cuesta for her ability, diligence, and kindness in all the hard work associated with preparing the manuscript and to Josephine Costa for her equally able and enthusiastic delivery of the many difficult and complicated secretarial and administrative tasks. I want to thank my wife, Sylvia, for her most helpful comments and enduring support.

*Philosophy in a New Key: A Study in the Symbolism of Reason, Rite and Art, 3rd edition (Cambridge, Mass.: Harvard University Press, 1979, p. xv).

CONTENTS

INTRODUCTION

"Are you happy?"

That's what I recently asked a seasoned colleague and friend. I expected not a simple no answer but a qualified yes, as I had gotten from the many others to whom I had posed this question in the past.

"I guess I am as happy as one can be, given what is going on in the world," he replied dismissively.

"And prior to now?" He was obviously reluctant.

"Well, you know I have a good job—though I could use a little more money; I have a great wife—though she could make a little more time for me; I have great children—though they could be a little more thoughtful; I am in good health—though I could do without the migraines and heartburn and a few other daily aggravations."

"Such as?"

"My mother—she is neither dying nor living: she is too old, too sick, too cranky, and, in all honesty, too expensive; and my 'old house'—something is always going wrong, either the roof leaks or the air conditioning doesn't work; the maid doesn't show up; the repair people don't do their jobs. And when all is well, the burglar alarm goes off spontaneously. Don't let me go on," he said with an exasperated voice.

"So, you are *not* really happy!"

"Well, it depends what do you mean by *happiness*."

Yes, what do we mean by happiness? How do we continue, never mind be "happy," when the adversities in life—

enormous or minor—seem overwhelming? How do we psychologically survive the major calamities in the world—man-made or natural? How do we face the loss of a loved one, serious illness, and impending death and still find meaning and happiness in life? The answers to all these questions lie in being a *grown-up, soulful, and spiritual person*.

André Malraux, the French novelist, described a country priest who had heard confessions for many decades and summed up what he had learned about human nature in two statements: "First of all, people are much more unhappy than one thinks . . . and second, there is no such thing as a grown-up person." These two observations are very closely related, if not one and the same: people who have not grown up cannot cultivate their souls and spirits, and therefore remain chronically susceptible to unhappiness.

The happiness that we all yearn for is a sentiment commonly associated with the lost paradise of our childhood—when we felt omnipotent, entitled, and immortal. Happiness in adulthood, however, requires realism, reciprocity, and coming to terms with one's mortality. It is cultivation of forgiveness, tolerance, patience, generosity, and compassion. If this sounds more like "sainthood" than adulthood, it is because "the first step toward spiritual growth," in the words of Scott Peck, is "growing up."

People seek happiness everywhere, except where it may be found. They acquire material possessions, money, and power, and at times explore the avenues of therapy and analysis, or even medication. They try to work through their past and present conflicts, develop insight and empathy, pull out their pathological anchorings, cuddle their inner child, and redesign their outer adult. They attend inspiring workshops and read sundry self-help books dealing with the meaning of life and secular spirituality. Candlelight dinners, gifts, and communication from the heart, however, go only so far. Some people try to find comfort in the structure of religion. Others cannot tolerate the rituals and specific prescriptions, repetitive sermons, and literalness of religionism. Some devote themselves to Buddhism and the like; others find such practices incongruent with their culture and religious background, and they drop out. Yet even the failures of all of these attempts are relative successes, though transient, as each attempt opens the door for another: the seeking itself generates hope.

Nonetheless, those unsatisfied always have a feeling that something is missing; some "thing" they cannot easily articulate that always escapes them. Though not totally sure, they suspect that the "thing" has to do with an ill-defined happiness. They search for life grounding in old and New Age philosophies, struggle between an existential void and pessimism, and experiential refills. They get married and divorced, have love affairs, experiment with drugs and alcohol, change jobs and towns.

With each of these changes, they find that vague unhappiness and restlessness seem to decline temporarily, but a gnawing, hollowing dysphoria always returns. Some of these people are therapists, counselors, rabbis, priests, ministers, or philosophers themselves. They are even more demoralized by the fact that their profession doesn't make them any better. This vague discomfort isn't limited to any specific group. Most of my friends, students, patients, and acquaintances try to speak about similar feelings whenever they allow themselves to be vulnerable to me. I know exactly what they are all talking about, for I have been there myself.

The "thing" that everyone is yearning for is not mere ordinary and transient happiness but rather an extraordinary and permanent joyful serenity. Psychologically, it is a state of fully grown-up adulthood anchored in a soulful and spiritual existence. The door to this state of mind can be opened only by a combination key involving both the soul and the spirit. It involves the soul through love: the love of others, the love of work, and the love of belonging. It involves the spirit through believing: believing in the sacred, believing in unity, and believing in transformation. All culminate in the belief in and love of God.

There is no easy or quick path to happiness, only a slow and arduous one toward it, as there is neither an end product nor a finishing line, only a starting point. In your quest for joyful serenity, there is no single spot where you can start. Where you are right now is the best place to begin.

THE WAY OF SOUL IS LOVE

———◆———

THE LOVE OF OTHERS

THE LOVE OF WORK

THE LOVE OF BELONGING

THE LOVE OF OTHERS

SELF-LOVE PRECEDES THE LOVE OF OTHERS

When Lisa, a twenty-eight-year-old, smart, beautiful, successful actress, walked into my office, fixed her big green eyes on me, and began to cry, I wondered what on earth could be making her so miserable. I knew a few, if distorted, things about her from the tabloids regularly displayed at my supermarket checkout counters. In between her uncontrollable sobs, she managed to say that she was very unhappy— unhappy with her choice of men, who all want to change her; unhappy with her career, in which she is reduced to a mouthpiece by a bunch of cynical writers; unhappy with her family, who take and take and are never satisfied. But most of all, she said, "I am unhappy about who I am and what I have become. I should not have been born, or I should not have been born as a human, maybe as a cat. In the next life, that is what I am shooting for. My cat and I are in perfect harmony. My cat seems to be the only one who has no complaints about me and me of her. Even my therapist thinks that I have a well-hidden inner bitch, and therefore am too narcissistically vulnerable. I just don't want to live anymore. Maybe I don't deserve to live, for I am such a bad person. I seem to be always irritable, angry, or depressed. Why should anyone bother to live with someone like me? Why should I bother to live? People who know me from my TV show might think that I am such a sunny person. They have no idea of my darker side. If they knew, they wouldn't want any part of me, because even I don't want myself, this totally selfish person."

I asked her how she had arrived at that conclusion that she was a selfish person. She said her boyfriend Joe had left her after a year and a half, because she was a "selfish bitch," an abnormal person, too self-absorbed to be a wife, especially a mother. Although she was somewhat hurt by the breakup, it was about time, because, she said, "he was too demanding. Plus, he always smelled of bubble gum, which he chewed to hide the smell of cigarettes. I don't know which I disliked more." Nevertheless, his reason for the breakup totally ungrounded her. Worst of all, she thought he might be right, and she remembered that even her own mother had accused her of being selfish throughout her childhood. In fact, her mother has used the same derogatory words as did Joe. "I don't even know who I am, or what I am anymore."

I asked her to give me some examples of her selfishness, as Joe or she saw it. "Well," said Lisa, "here is the most recent incident that actually prompted the breakup. I got an offer to work on a movie in L.A., which unfortunately coincides, time-wise, with our long-planned vacation to Alaska. I discussed this with him, the importance of the offer for my career, and that we could reschedule our vacation. I was torn myself. But I finally chose to accept the offer. There we are. Yes, I am selfish; he is right. Some other woman would have chosen the relationship over this specific opportunity; chose marriage, home, children over the career. I mean, Joe is a normal person, he wants a wife."

I asked her why his demand that she choose what he wants makes him less selfish. She stopped crying. In fact, I said, "both of you are quite selfish"—she burst into laughter—"but in a good sense of the word. You both have your 'selves' to take care of. You have the right and the responsibility to love and to protect yourself. Your choices are part of that self, which needs and deserves respect and self-compassion."

Self-love is benign self-compassion, not malignant self-centeredness, which unfortunately we call narcissism. Narcissism refers to a metaphor that describes a particular state of mind in which the world appears as a mirror of the self. It is used as an expression of unprincipled self-preoccupation. Even at that level of reading, as Thomas Moore says, "Narcissus falls in love with his image [and] discovers by his own experience that he is lovable." We tolerate better, and in fact find warmness in, such self-love when we see it in children.

This positive view of the myth of Narcissus tells a story of transformation through self-love. The word *narcissism* derives from the classical Greek myth, in which the main character, a youth called Narcissus, falls in love with himself. The child, in fact, is so beautiful that not only he but everyone else is in love with him. In his self-absorption, he is unable to relate to anyone, never mind being able to love another. The closest he gets to anyone is to a nymph (ironically called Echo), who can only repeat what she hears. She becomes a mere voice reflecting him. Isolated and unengaged, he gazes at his own image in the water and yearns only for himself. As he reaches down to touch his reflection, he disappears into the abyss of the waters of the river Styx. Ultimately what remains in his place is a flower, a yellow-centered daffodil with white petals—the narcissus. Although Western psychology generally interprets the myth as Narcissus drowning in his own pathology, in fact the story has less to do with being destroyed by one's self-preoccupation than with the ultimate salvation inherent even within the most desperate of us. It is the story of transformation from one form of nature to another—a boy who becomes a flower. In such a transformation, the boy becomes a part of a larger whole.

In self-love, there is a potential for being part of the whole. In this sense, self-love engenders a feeling of union with the rest of nature. It is a mutual self-love, a form of communion among all creatures. This is a merciful self-love, healthy narcissism and, far from being pathological, it is very much needed as a basic ingredient for attachment to and love of others.

THERE IS GOOD ONLY BECAUSE THERE IS BAD

Birds make great sky-circles of their freedom.
How do they learn it?
They fall, and falling, they're given wings.

—Jalālu'l-Dīn Rūmi

That evening, less than ten hours after breaking up with her, Joe called Lisa and wanted to bring some take-out food to her place. Lisa was elated. She put back into the refrigerator a six-pack of Joe's favorite beer, which she had removed earlier. She wasn't going to allow some cheap beer she would never serve to her friends to occupy space in her refrigerator. Joe walked in with only two boxes of Chinese food. No flowers, or any other sign or gesture in recognition of their coming together after a painful day of his rejection of her. She, meanwhile, welcomed him powdered and totally naked except for one of his bright red ties. His first reaction was anger: "You ruined my tie! Now the powder will never come off. You know I paid eighty dollars for it, you fool!"

Lisa felt horrible. She had been so excited while she was preparing herself for him. "He will be so pleasantly surprised that we'll forget the food and jump into each other's arms," she joyfully expected. Instead she got a serious scolding, disapproval and anger. Not only did he not want to make love but he didn't even want to sit down to eat. He spent the next half hour on the balcony shaking his tie violently to get rid of the powder while talking with someone on the cellular phone. How could I be so wrong? she thought. She tried to shake off the powder, but he wouldn't let her do it. "I'll buy you another one. I am sorry, I wanted to entertain you after we had such a horrible day. Can you at least acknowledge that it was sexy, or well-intentioned? I mean, am I crazy, totally out of it?" Joe wouldn't respond. She kept begging for some recognition. He remained disapprovingly silent. Joe would have equally rejected Erasmus, who stresses in his *Praise of Folly* that intimacy develops through the appreciation of foolishness.

Lisa, by contrast, never minded tolerating such explicit rejection and would go around to sniff hints of it. She was always seeking self-validation. Not only couldn't she stand people disagreeing with her, because disagreement fed into her self-doubt, but she also wanted to be liked by everyone, especially by people she disliked. At a party, if everyone was friendly toward her except one individual, she would gravitate toward the unfriendly one and try to obtain some sign of acceptance or approval. Her friends never understood why she would spend most of her time with utterly obnoxious and unlikable people at every gathering, professional and social. Lisa couldn't tolerate the idea that self-validation requires being rejected by some. Confucius was asked, "Is it best that all the people of the village like a person?" "No," he replied. "It is best when the good people of the village like him, and the bad people of the village dislike him."

Lisa would come home from such parties or meetings unhappy and disturbed, because she wouldn't have gotten the validation she required from these unvalidating characters. She thought that by some "karma" she was drawn to such bad, rejecting, negating people and would recite at length the awful experiences she had had with them. But in fact what was happening was much less mysterious. She came from an enmeshed and negating household. She was drawn to similar people and feelings as a home base, however painful. Noah benShea's book *The Word: Jewish Wisdom Through Time* tells a Yiddish folktale that shows how where we came from and to whom we may want to go affect our predisposition:

> *An old man sat outside the walls of a great city. When travelers approached they would ask the old man: "What kind of people live in this city?" And the old man would answer: "What kind of people lived in the place where you came from?" If the travelers answered: "Only bad people lived in the place where we came from." Then the old man would reply: "Continue on, you will find only bad people here." But if the travelers answered: "Only good people lived in the place where we have come from." Then the old man would say: "Enter, for here, too, you will find only good people."*

This story, in order to make its point of the powerful influence of past experiences on the present, polarizes "good" and "bad" as distinct entities. In reality, such a distinction rarely exists. People in Lisa's present life were neither all angels nor all monsters. Those awful people from whom she sought approval were also most likely rejected, insecure, anxious, or in some other ways troubled themselves. So were her parents.

There are no such things as good people or bad people as Lisa tried to classify them. There is only goodness and badness delivered by individuals. Some people do more good than bad, and some more bad than good. "Badness" and "goodness" define human beings and are often opposite sides of the same coin. As the wisdom of Lao Tzu says, "If goodness is taken as goodness, wickedness enters as well," to achieve that which characterizes much of the world. To cultivate the good and eliminate the bad is as unlikely as to have an electric current without both positive and negative poles. It is better to accept the principle of polarity—plus-minus, north-south, sky-earth, passion-reason (and indeed all pairs of opposites), because they are really different aspects of one and the same system. These two alternative forces, or phases, in the rhythm of everything in the Universe have been portrayed as Yin and Yang. The disappearance of either of them would mean the disappearance of the whole.

Lisa's "stingy Joe" was the same Joe who gave a lavish surprise party for her twenty-seventh birthday in one of the most expensive restaurants in town and bought her a Tiffany pearl necklace. This "rigid Joe" was the same Joe who was willing to convert should they get married, if she so desired. This "unforgiving Joe" was the same Joe who didn't get angry when he contracted genital warts from her and after the first eruption never mentioned it again.

Things are never black and white, or black or white; they are black-white. In Lao Tzu's *Tao Te Ching* (*Way of Life*), under heaven all can see beauty as beauty only because there is ugliness; there is good only because there is evil. How often are we surprised to find out that a person who is known to us as a good individual did something horrifying. Is it our poor judgment, our lack of intuition or knowledge, or was he so deceptive and duplicitous? None of these. He was always himself, a good person, who did a bad thing, or what we personally or collectively called a bad thing. Is divorcing a spouse after fifteen years of marriage a bad thing, or an honest thing though belatedly executed? Are donations tax-related incentives, or genuine charities? Are missionaries saints, or are their activities serving primarily to define themselves? Independent of the possibly mixed motives of individuals, donations and missionary services are useful contributions to the community. There are good things whether they were executed by good people or not-so-good people, or bad people or not-so-bad people, or good-bad people, or just people.

Marianne Williamson relates a memorable anecdote about the great Italian painter Leonardo da Vinci that reveals the invisible connections between these dualities:

> *Early in his career, he was painting a picture of Christ, and found a profoundly beautiful young male to model for his portrait of Jesus. Many years later he walked through the streets of Florence looking for the perfect person to portray the great betrayer. Finally he found someone dark-looking enough to do the job. He went up to the man to approach him to do the modeling. The man looked at him and said, "You don't remember me, but I know you. Years ago, I was the model for your picture of Jesus."*

THE SEARCH FOR COMPLETION OF
SELF IN OTHERS IS PURSUIT OF
WHOLENESS, NOT LOVE

As much as Lisa needed some distance from people to feel independent, Joe needed others very close to feel whole. Lisa maintained her sanity by keeping away from her engulfing mother, who was still alive. Joe came from a divorced family. His mother left the family when he was four years old and lived with a man in the neighborhood. Joe shuffled between two houses but never really found a home. He maintained his sanity by clinging to his independent mother, who had died three years ago from breast cancer. Joe made statements to Lisa like these: "I want you to be with me"; "Nothing should compete with our completing each other"; "The more you assert your individuality, the less chance that we could ever merge and be soul mates."

Loving someone doesn't mean merging with that person. The myth of Hermaphrodite tried to explain why we human beings are so predisposed to merge with our lovers (not necessarily urging that we should or must do so in order to find true love, or even that merging is a desirable thing to strive for).

In Plato's famous dialogue *Symposium,* Aristophanes decided to help his friends learn the secret of love's power. He began by recalling the myth that human beings were originally hermaphrodites: each human combined two genders by being a rounded whole, with four legs and four arms, able to walk upright in either direction, or to run by turning over and over in circular fashion. These original dual-sex human beings were so strong, confident, and powerful that they became a major threat to the gods, who debated how best to reduce their power. Zeus decided that they should be bisected and arranged it so that reproduction would take place by means of sexual intercourse (instead of by emission onto the ground, as had occurred previously). The result of this division was profound: Each half-being felt compelled to seek out a partner who would restore its former wholeness. Love, concluded Aristophanes, is simply the name for the desire and pursuit of the whole. Similarly, in the Kabbala, Shekinah is God's feminine half, who hopes to unite with the masculine half.

Throughout the ages, the idea that we attain wholeness and complete ourselves by merging sexually with someone else has been the major inspiration of romantic literature and the stirring climax of countless novels about love, often at the expense of enduring relationships.

Joe's desire was not to relate to Lisa but to *merge with* her, which she experienced as a sort of psychological cannibalism. Such an urge is not being with the other person but actually being the other. In this sense it is self-annihilation, expressing only Joe's intolerance of separateness. This intolerance generates a variety of manifestations. Alone, it engenders ungluing anxiety; with another, it is an intolerable, domineering attitude and demanding dependency. Paradoxically, the more the male dominates, as Joe was trying to do with Lisa, the more dependent he becomes. To a greater and greater extent, the relationship takes on qualities of the mother-infant bond, which in turn results in greater fear of separation and even greater domination. In adulthood the male-master becomes excessively dependent on his female-slave, and the female-slave grows to love her chains because of her hidden power over the master. Meanwhile, their wholeness becomes embedded in the context of mutual self-negation. Lisa's "selfishness" is her desperate attempt to put some obstacle in front of this seemingly inevitable recruitment by Joe, while she is intrigued by the hidden power it carries for her.

PRIMAL NEED TO MERGE
INTERFERES WITH RELATIONSHIPS

We bake a lump of clay,
Molded into a figure of you
And a figure of me.
Then we take both of them,
And break them into pieces,
And mix the pieces with water,
And mold again a figure of you,
And a figure of me.
I am in your clay.
You are in my clay.
In life we share a single quilt.
In death we will share one coffin.

—Kuan Tao-Sheng

Our prenatal state is one of total fusion with a pregnant female. The mother basically breathes and eats for her growing fetus. The fetus is not differentiated from the uterus, which receives all of its nutrients from its arteries, while its toxic elements are removed through its veins. Naturally, whatever the female is doing for her uterus and its contents, the fetus, she is doing for herself. All is a single entity. But at some point in gestation (approximately three months) the fetus's brain starts to receive information from its own parts. As it matures, it will experience tactile and auditory sensations, as well as differentiate internal from external stimuli.

Until then the fetus lives in a nondifferentiated, merged state of passive calmness. This blissful state is imprinted and remembered in our minds and bodies as the most secure and most peaceful existence, rendering us incarnates of longing. For the remainder of our lives, we long for this soothing state in its innumerable forms and situations, either directly and primitively trying to enter women's inner space or less primitively and indirectly seeking transitional objects. The term *transitional objects,* in fact, has been adopted to refer to substitute external objects (not part of the body) to soothe the infant, such as blankets or bibs, soft toys (like the classic teddy bear), certain clothing and familiar objects, even people who may function as surrogate soothers to whom babies may connect when anxious. Joe wanted Lisa to be his transitional object, but permanently, even though she was neither satisfactory for the role nor willing to accept it.

Our transitional objects are clear agents of continuity, as the sociologist Eviatar Zerubavel explains, constituting bridges between the self and the world. They help the child to feel connected at the same time that it is experiencing its most devastating separation. Dolls and stuffed animals allow the baby to separate from its mother while they are experientially embedded in the immediate environment. As intermediaries between "me" and "not me," they help to establish an ambiguous, transitional zone between the self and the world, permitting the child to feel simultaneously separate and connected. We can easily observe that adults in everyday life can also cling (literally as well as metaphorically) to transitional objects no longer associated with babyhood—mechanical objects like a CD player or cell phone, or even a car—as expressions of a strong emotional need to feel attached to something.

Children don't give up their transitional objects—nor should they be forced or cajoled to do so—until they are developmentally ready, that is, only after they have the capacity to attach to others without fusing with them.

While Joe was looking for permanency, continuity, and connectedness by fusing with Lisa, she was trying to prevent fusion, as if they were tuning in different frequencies. She had had that with her mother and wasn't about to repeat the kind of enmeshment from which she'd spent a fortune to recover. Her last therapist had encouraged her to be totally independent and implicitly discouraged her from trusting men. This is a rather pessimistic view of the world, as it pins one to the past permanently. People grow, mature, or at least change; so do circumstances. Lisa's past may predispose her to certain conceptions, perceptions, and repetitions, as in the Yiddish tale I mentioned earlier, but they need not determine her actions. Heraclitus contends that one cannot step in the same river twice, because no one thing is ever the same thing twice. One may not step in the same river twice not merely because the river flows and changes but also because the one who steps into it continually changes as well.

At the opposite end of enmeshment, there exists an equally conflict-creating pattern of non-relating. Some people simply don't relate. I don't mean those with certain neurophysiological handicaps, such as autism or schizoid personality. There are individuals who do not consider relating to another person, never mind making the relationship a priority, important enough to invest their time and psychic energy. Relegating the relation to secondary significance is not limited to spouses. These non-relaters treat everyone (parents, children, friends) similarly. This stance may be to some extent tolerated with very creative people, but even then it is at a high cost to the individuals involved. However different from one another they may be in their personal lives, these creative people share an enormous capacity for original work—often accompanied by a lack of close relationships with other human beings. Some may, in fact, logically argue that, if they have very intimate engagement with their families and friends, their singular achievements would be compromised, if not impossible. The heights of creativity demand long periods of solitude and intense concentration, which are difficult to maintain if a person is to engage emotionally with a spouse, children, or others. Creative people usually merge with their work, not with another person, in order to complete their selves. They mirror themselves on a canvas, or on a blank sheet of writing paper, or on a laboratory table. When they marry, their spouses no doubt chronically complain of being lonely, even in their "presence." A less tolerated version of this relegating of relationships to secondary importance is frequently observed with successful businesspeople and professionals.

LOVE IS CELEBRATING OTHERS' DIFFERENCES,
CONFUSIONS, AND PECULIARITIES WITHOUT
EXPECTING THEY BE LIKE US—"NORMAL"

Ring the bells that still can ring,
Forget your perfect offering.
There is a crack in everything.
That's how the light gets in.

—Leonard Cohen

One afternoon, according to thirteenth-century Sufi folktale, the beloved character Nasreddin, a humorous philosopher and wise fool, was sitting in a café with his friend, discussing serious matters of life and love, as told to Rick Fields.

> *When the friend asked if Nasreddin was ever interested in getting married, he replied that years before he had set out to find the perfect wife. In Damascus he had found a wonderful and beautiful woman—but she wasn't spiritual enough. Then, in another city he found a spiritual woman, but they didn't communicate well together. Ultimately, in Cairo he found what he was looking for— "She was the ideal woman, spiritual, gracious, beautiful and at ease in the world—perfect in every way." When the friend asked why he hadn't married her, Nasreddin replied, "Unfortunately, she was looking for the perfect man."*

Both Joe and Lisa wanted the other one to be perfect while rigorously denying their desire. Furthermore, they were putting themselves up as such examples of perfection. She would assail him for his crib talk and priapic preoccupation, and would complain of his always trading information. "Why do you always wear dark grays and blacks? You want to be able to show up at a funeral at a moment's notice?" He would criticize her for her "vagina talk," psychological decadence, and verbal bewitchment, and would complain of her always trading people. "Why don't you wear a bra? At a moment's notice you want to be able to get into the sack?" They didn't yet know that personal imperfections are what make one lovable.

When we refer to the perfect person, what we may really mean is someone resembling ourselves. That is why it is so difficult to find the perfect one, because each of us is unique. The people we encounter are to varying degrees different from ourselves. In fact, rewording the esteemed thirteenth-century monk, Thomas Aquinas, "Diversity is the only perfection in the universe." As there are billions of different faces in the world, there are that many variations in human personalities. "I" as the norm is puzzled and confused if the other behaves differently from "me." We automatically expect the other person's psychological structure to be similar to our own. Yet the moment a difference is recognized, however small, the individual would likely pull back, either remain relatively distant or emulate the other. Both attempts interfere with the development of intimacy. Genuine intimate relationships require that both individuals accept and foster each other's separateness. This acceptance is not a form of tolerance—it is a celebration. We should *not* be hoping that one day this person will finally mature and become like ourselves.

To know a man as he really is, you must accept him as he is; otherwise, he may not reveal himself to you and you will miss him forever. Constant self-scrutiny as to be rational, perfect, sane, or praiseworthy undermines one's authenticity, and thus the possibility of genuine relations with others. Irrationalities are fertile ground for souls to join, as are their shortcomings and failures. Enduring relations are a series of optimum failures. If you want successful relations, make a habit of practicing the following daily prayer from the Course in Miracles: "Today, I shall judge nothing."

SOULFUL INTIMACY IS THE PROTECTION OF THE PRIVACY OF THE OTHER

Joe's excessive clinging is the most frequent manifestation of structured emotional dependence on another person, which is often taken for love. Such intense and intractable attachments, however, invariably lack the very ingredients required for genuine love—delight in the other person in his or her own right and in the person's own way as an independent being. The kind of love Joe professes is a counterfeit love and tends to deprive his partner of a life of her own. Such people's love does not even discriminate among partners; having love needs met becomes more important than who meets them. This motivation harkens back again to the infant-mother relationship, in which one is not interested in *who* provides the milk and sings the lullaby as long as someone does. For Joe, a Lisa is needed not as someone to relate to; she is needed to fill his inner emptiness.

Healthy attachment requires healthy distance. A healthy distance is accomplished by allowing, if not making sure, that one's partner's separateness is secured. The poet Rainer Maria Rilke's advice for a happy relationship is for each person to protect the solitude of the other, never mind his own. Only by being separate can one be together.

SOULFULNESS IS NOT BLAMING

Lisa and Joe constantly blamed each other, even for inconsequential matters. He expected total loyalty. If he had an argument with a waiter in a restaurant or with a cabdriver, he expected her to support him, regardless of whether he was right. Any failings of her support were considered utter disloyalty. She blamed him for being satisfied with trickled down analyses from her, not knowing acts of emotional intimacy, such as hugging, kissing, or cuddling, except as quick foreplay for self-affirmatory sex. And there was not even a pretense of afterplay. He'd turn over and snore. "He doesn't communicate, share his inner thoughts, his demons," as she put it. He, in return, accused her confusing living with being in therapy and "genderlect" conversations. He blamed her for his own reticence about his inner world. What's more, as soon as he did so, she would attack him, accuse him of perversity, and demand that he see a therapist, one with gravitas, rather than a "lite therapist." A therapist of transpersonal persuasion that he reluctantly agreed to visit discharged him after the first session by saying, "You are not OK, I am not OK, and it is OK."

Both wanted to know more about each other but got upset with each finding. He was jealous of her intense interest in musicians and her taking voice lessons with a gay woman. She was upset by his bringing work home on weekends.

Lisa's and Joe's chronic complaints about each other didn't help much in changing their behaviors. They served only to lower the couple's threshold of psychological vulnerability, and gave rise to anger and rage. People are at their best and worst when in love. At their worst moments, Joe and Lisa called each other all kinds of names. She was a "NutraSweet" soul and a "hothouse lesbo"; he was an "id-ridden asshole" and a "zoo-raised lion." They threw things at each other; he shook her, she bit him. After these fights, escalated by the contagion of anger, they would remain aloof or continue to accuse each other and eventually make up in bed, but never explicitly apologize. Implicitly they accepted that the passion ensued from transgression.

Most arguments escalate between spouses, other family members, friends, or co-workers because no one takes the blame and says, "It is my fault, and I am sorry." An apology could end even major wars among nations, never mind the ordinary arguments of individuals. Commonly, people accuse someone else for whatever has gone wrong, and there may be a small truth in that projection. But the accused's insistence that he is only an innocent bystander, if not the victim, is usually perceived by others as an insult to their intelligence, a maneuver that compounds the original wrongdoing. There may be a deeper reason, in fact an ontological one, for this universal defense of not accepting blame. It goes all the way back to Genesis in the Bible, when God put Adam in the Garden of Eden and commanded him never to eat from the tree of knowledge of good and evil. When Adam hid from God because he didn't want to be seen naked, God wondered how Adam knew that he was naked and asked, "Did you eat fruit from the tree of knowledge I commanded you not to eat from?" He answered, "That woman, the one you gave me, gave me some fruit from the tree and I ate it." Then the Lord God asked the woman, "What have you done?" "The snake deceived me," the woman answered.

Adam, in fact, not only blamed the woman for giving him the fruit but also blamed God for giving him the woman. And the woman accused the snake and blamed God, the snake's creator, indirectly. Incidentally, God never bothered to ask the snake what happened. We can only speculate that the serpent itself would have blamed someone or something else, most likely the tree, and indirectly God. If we cannot blame someone easily identifiable, we all directly or indirectly blame God for our failings. God has no one to blame. Becoming soulful means becoming God-like, thus not blaming others even when justified, and also accepting the unjustified blame from others who may still need to blame.

DO NOT SHED TOO MUCH
LIGHT ON THE SOUL

One always learns one's mystery at the price of one's innocence.

—Robertson Davies

At the beginning, Joe and Lisa had a fully satisfying sexual relationship. As time passed, they had to invent little games to get themselves excited. But each would insist that the other come up with an intriguing scenario. Finally, they'd throw a coin, and the loser would proceed with a story. In one of Lisa's stories, she was a maid to Sir Joe, an English lord, who was sitting in an oversized leather chair, reading a newspaper while sipping a cognac, smoking a cigar, totally oblivious to her comings and goings as she tidied the place. She would get closer and closer to his area, take his slippers off, pull down his pajama bottoms, wash his genitals, dry them with her little apron, and then suck him until he came. Meanwhile, the lord wasn't supposed to make any change in his routine, as he continued reading, sipping, and smoking, even at the time of his ejaculation.

Although Lisa guessed and delivered accurately Joe's fantasy, she'd go into a funk afterward, and if Joe pursued her with "what's wrong" questions, she'd berate him about the impersonal quality of his sexuality, the interchangeability of "the server." She would demand to know in detail what went on in his mind during all his acting, to which he'd respond, "Honestly, nothing." "Nothing? Nothing?" she'd scream. First she couldn't believe that and accuse him of lying. Then, if halfway convinced, she would attack him with pity, saying that he was just empty-headed, a bore.

"How can we have an intimate relationship when you are always hiding from me?"

"Doctor, does that make me a bad person?" Joe asked. "The situation is a little like the final scene in the Wizard of Oz, when Dorothy unmasks the powerful wizard as a mere mortal, old and bald, and accuses him of being a bad person. The Wizard replies that he is really a good person, even though he may be a bad wizard. Like the Wizard, I am a good person, but not a good communicator. At times I don't even know enough about myself to communicate to Lisa."

Intimacy doesn't require absolute knowledge of oneself or the other person. There is always some resistance to too much self-exploration. People really don't want to know or have it known what secrets are slumbering in their souls. If you try too much to penetrate another person, you'll find that you have thrust him into a defensive position that he fights against. In fact, the knowledge of the other is best initiated not by exploration but by a simple declaration: You are fine as you are. Of course, in order to offer such acceptance to another, one has to accept oneself. Such self-acceptance requires the acknowledgment and ownership of a bad as well as a good side of self, one's hidden darkness or shadow.

The shadow may include our anger, selfishness, jealousy, pride, insecurity, wildness, or destructiveness. Although these qualities are an integral part of us, we want to hide them or deny them. They get out of the darkness when we project them onto others—husband, wife, child, friend, neighbor, co-worker, or another race and culture. Only by accepting one's own shadow can one allow the other person to keep his own secrets.

Stripping the other person of his depth and psychological secrets is not getting to know someone. In fact, getting to know someone deeply would require not seeing too clearly. The magic in relationships is maintained partly by taming one's excessive curiosity to discover the ingredients of the whole, by resisting unweaving the mystery of otherness, by not throwing too much light on the person. Every soul has "a lie" in its formation, because it is never fully formed; at any given stage, it seems like pretending. Dr. Relling, in Ibsen's *Wild Duck,* says that he takes care to preserve his life lie. If you take away the average person's "life lie," you rob him of his happiness too.

The need not to shed too much light on another person harkens back to ancient Greek mythology—the beautiful princess Psyche and her beloved Eros (Cupid). Psyche was unable to find a husband, but an oracle revealed that a monster on top of a mountain would marry her. Unbeknownst to Psyche, that beast was really Eros, whom she had promised never to look upon. Convinced by her jealous sisters to break that vow, she lit a lamp and beheld the handsome Eros as he slept. Suddenly awakened and realizing that he had been betrayed, the winged figure flew away.

Of course, Eros was Love.

ALL TRIANGULATIONS DESERVE
JEALOUSY AND CELEBRATION

*If you love one, you will be loved by many, but
if you love many, you'll incur the wrath of one.*

Not only was Lisa pretty but she also worked in a setting where everyone was chosen for attractiveness, physical or psychological—mostly physical. They also had many parties, and seemed to have lots of fun, in contrast to Joe's dry, driven world of money, wherein a party meant getting together with people to make deals, which were drawing much emotional blood from Lisa. He'd go to her parties only to come home to fight. "Why do you have to touch people caressingly?" he would complain. And "what is that seductive curling of your lips whenever you talk to your boss? Are you sleeping with him? You would, if need be," he would conclude with the not-so-well disguised self-pity of a jealous lover. On such nights they would sleep in different rooms.

But whenever Joe went on a business trip, he was accompanied by an assistant, or a junior colleague, mostly women, especially one Lisa called "a scheming type." "What do they talk about during dinner?" she would wonder. "Do they share a bottle of wine? Does the maître d' treat them as lovers? Do they taste each other's food? I can almost see her extending her fork to Joe's lips, 'Oh! You've got to taste this.' Joe would roll it in his mouth and look into her eyes, 'It is delicious.'" Lisa would so elaborate her fantasies that she'd call Joe at his hotel and break up with him.

Both Joe and Lisa were like many other people, who are very jealous and provoke such feelings in each other. Nevertheless, they refused to admit having these feelings because of the demeaning implications of such an admission. In reality, jealousy is corrosive only if left unattended. Otherwise, it is a natural human emotion and, as such, a building block of one's soul. One needs to recognize its archetypal existence, understand its nature, chip away its sharp edges, attend to it, and put it to good use.

Jealousy has the potential of converting to an obsession. When that conversion occurs, no preemptive dismissal helps, nor does reassurance or the advice of friends, the admonishment of others, the threat of punishment, the danger of loss of prestige, dignity, reputation, marriage, even life. What kind of madness would let a person take such a destructive and self-destructive road? That person could, in fact, be very sane, well-educated, well-bred, extremely intelligent, highly sophisticated, someone who holds a major office, or is a respected community leader. We have seen judges, teachers, doctors, and ministers become victims of jealousy and act on it, destroying their careers, if not their lives, as well as the lives of their loved ones.

Biological sources of jealousy are conditional, designed to protect the territory for food and, ultimately, to perpetuate one's genes. Studies of primates show how their "jealous behavior" carries the clear mark of evolutionary purposes. In a discussion of the reproductive strategies of the male, Kalman Glantz and John K. Pearce observe:

> Males are most vigilant when their females are in estrus. At other times, they are much more tolerant. A dominant (silver-back) male keeps a constant vigil on the movements of his mates as long as they are not pregnant. However, once a female has conceived, he becomes incredibly tolerant. He may watch, from a distance of several feet, while the future mother of his offspring copulates enthusiastically with another silver-back. A female may well indulge in more sexual acts, sometimes including homosexual mounts, during the early months of her pregnancy than during her estrus period. A pregnant gorilla can quite literally do no wrong.

Man's jealousy exceeds these biological restraints, and woman's jealousy has no counterpart in other mammals. In humans, it seems, the seeds of jealousy are sown originally in the archetypal triangulation. They are resown in early childhood, to be reenacted later in peer relationships and love affairs. In all these relations, one of the individuals (at times both) begins to lose his or her boundaries, is unable to tolerate the other's independent activities, never mind another love affair. To some extent, a real or fantasied third person is needed to fuel a dormant interest. At times lovers consciously or unconsciously play that game to incite passion. However, to keep the triangulation at the level of foreplay requires that the couple maintain a certain degree of introspective distance from their emotions. If such differentiation and distance are lost, the couple will be at the mercy of a drama of mythical proportions.

The story of Aphrodite gives us the archetypical triangulated jealousy. Feeling denied by Hippolytus, who seems to be favoring Artemis, Aphrodite sets out to destroy him. Her rage brings her lover an ironic death by being trampled by his horses, which were an object of his intense love.

Lots of marriages end up in divorce simply because they go through the neglect-anger-suspicion-jealousy-humiliation sequence, eroding trust and impoverishing the couple's souls. Finally, divorce becomes the only viable way to escape from this vicious, mutually depleting cycle, even though the partners may still be very much in love. Transient love affairs of married individuals generate terrible pain but do not necessarily precipitate divorce, if this vicious cycle is not allowed to be entrenched in the relationship.

THE SELFISH SAINT: TO FORGIVE IS TO FORGET

The mind has a thousand eyes, And the heart but one; Yet the light of a whole life dies, When love is done.

—Francis William Bourdillon

As Joe and Lisa were celebrating the second anniversary of their meeting, their relationship faced a serious and most damaging challenge. She found a package of lubricated condoms in his pocket. They never used protection because she was on birth control pills. Yes, she was snooping. It turned out she always did. Now they were in totally untested waters. She threw his clothes out the window of their apartment, then changed the locks on the door.

He called dozens of times, at home, at work, left desperate messages, proposing marriage on the one hand, denying that the condoms were his on the other, said he had no idea how they got into his pocket. He proposed an explanation: "Could someone be trying to sabotage our relationship, like your lesbian music teacher?" He sent dozens of red roses, parked in front of the apartment to talk to her. She would not respond. She spent the next few nights sleepless, in pain and anger. She couldn't believe that after all they have gone through, he could have sex with someone else. Why? Was she depriving him of sex? Was she not a good sexual partner? She wondered who the woman was. The schemer? "Obviously someone young, childbearing age, otherwise why use a condom? Or was he sleeping with prostitutes?" She wondered whether he had given her AIDS. As her anger dissipated and a darker mood set in, not only was she betrayed and humiliated but she had lost her friend. As much as she complained about him, Joe was the best friend she'd ever had. How could he do that to her, just for sex? Did she really miss him, she wondered, or was she simply growing dependent on her opponent? Actually pushing away pulls one in.

Ironically, through her lesbian teacher's mediation Lisa and Joe began to talk. He was deeply remorseful. He confessed that he had had sex twice with a waitress in their neighborhood restaurant. He liked her "adventurousness" in bed. But the real reason for his "sin" was, as his therapist saw it, his "cold feet," that he was trying to undermine the relationship, which was getting too close for comfort. Lisa finally forgave him and said, "But I'll never forget." I urged that she should also try to forget it, for her own sake. She tried, but she couldn't get rid of the images of his having sex with someone else. She knew the other woman too and thought she had a cute rear end. She was obsessed with what Joe meant by "the adventures in sex." Were they having anal intercourse? That may have explained the lubricated condoms, she thought. But no way would she do that herself. "To hell with him, if that's what he wants."

To love means to forgive, especially to forgive what seems unforgivable. Christ has always loved the sinner as being the nearest possible to the perfection of humanity. His primary desire was not to reform people any more than his desire was to relieve suffering.

Similarly, forgiveness is praised by philosophers and religious leaders alike as heroic existence. "Life is an adventure in forgiveness," declares Norman Cousins. "Have no malice in your heart. Have no desire for revenge," we read in the Hindu sacred poem the Bhagavad Gita. "Give the person a full chance to explain. Do not return hate." Jesus, a very brave man, prays while hanging on the cross of death, "Father, forgive them, for they know not what they do." Dr.

Martin Luther King, Jr., the African American civil rights leader adds, "Forgiveness is not an occasional act; it is a permanent attitude." Finally, the writer David Ausburger concludes: "Since nothing we intend is ever faultless, and nothing we attempt ever without error, and nothing we achieve without some measure of finitude and fallibility we call humanness, we are saved by forgiveness."

If your partner acknowledges his or her mistake, expresses sincere remorse and repents, then you must not only forgive him or her but also forget the whole event. After such contrition, the slate must be wiped clean and the relationship must continue as if the wrongdoing never occurred.

In his book *Further Along the Road Less Traveled,* M. Scott Peck tells a poignant tale about a little girl who said she talked to God.

> *The villagers who heard of her experience began to get excited about it, and word reached the bishop's palace. The bishop, concerned of unauthorized saints walking around, appointed a monsignor to investigate the child's story. So she was brought to the bishop's palace for a series of interviews. By the end of the third interview, the monsignor, in frustration, cried out, "I just don't know, I don't know what to make of this. I don't know whether you're for real or not. But there is one acid test. The next time you talk to God, I want you to ask Him what I confessed to at my last confession. Would you do that?" In reply, the little girl said she would do so. When she came back for her interview the following week, the monsignor eagerly asked, "So, my dear, did you talk to God again this past week?" to which she replied, "Yes, Father, I did." He went on, "And when you talked to God this past week, did you remember to ask Him what I confessed to at my last confession?" Again she answered, "Yes, Father, I did."*

Finally, he asked, "Well? When you asked God what I confessed to at my last confession, what did God say?" Then the little girl answered, "God said, I've forgotten."

Whether this little girl was the one who had forgotten, and whether she had indeed talked to God, she was expressing the ultimate forgiveness.

Humanness is always imperfect, relative, and tainted by sin and folly. This view might help us to tolerate our own shortcomings and many uncertainties, including our moral failings. Forgiving would free us from the corrosive effects of anger and hate. It would save relationships among spouses, parents and children, and friends. I know spouses who never forgive an indiscretion and express their anger at every reminder of it. They will yell at the top of their voices, as if the matter had just occurred. Such chronic anger serves only to kill the love that was supposed to be its source. It is reminiscent of Robert Fulghum's report of a unique practice in the Solomon Islands of the South Pacific. Applying a unique type of logging, some native woodsmen cut down trees by yelling at them. They continue this practice for thirty days, until each tree finally dies, believing that their screaming killed the spirit of the tree. The tree may or may not literally fall over. The person who is subjected to anger may or may not die. We know for certain, however, that anger slowly kills love.

Ironically, the angry one (justified or not) suffers the most. Not only will he or she lose the love that is so vehemently being protected but the anger will weaken the immunological system. Being angry, in fact, has been likened by Frederick Buechner to gnawing on a bone, your own. The moral of the story is that people who say, "I forgive, but I will never forget," have not actually forgiven. Forgetting is the only real and possible forgiving, and that is a more saintly act, and a selfish one at that.

EXPECT LIMITED LOYALTY, RECEIVE PLENTY

We expect lots of things from friends and family members, frequently get disappointed, but nevertheless recover and continue with our expectations. Disloyalty, though, is the harshest of all disappointments. Even a minor betrayal by a friend or loved one comes as a devastating blow and a major surprise. We are unable to believe it when we face squarely an act of betrayal by those from whom we expected complete loyalty; it shakes all our confidence in relationships and even in ourselves. We couldn't imagine ourselves doing such a heinous thing. But is it true that there are no conditions in which our own loyalty is not seriously challenged?

Like all human sentiments, loyalty is context-dependent. It is a relative commitment. It is our *expectation* that loyalty be absolute that generates disappointments, conflicts, and loss of important relationships. By recognizing human limitations, we might be able to salvage our connections and also have peacefulness within us. And in fact it is only by *not* expecting absolute loyalty that we may receive it. In the Book of Matthew, we learn the nature of loyalty. Jesus said to his disciples, "All of you will abandon me tonight." Peter said to him, "Even if everyone else abandons you, I never will." Jesus replied to Peter, "I can guarantee this truth: Before a rooster crows tonight, you will say three times that you don't know me." Peter told him, "Even if I have to die with you, I'll never say that I don't know you!" All the other disciples said the same thing, and they all deserted the man to whom they had sworn loyalty.

MARRIAGE IS AN INDIVIDUATION PROCESS
WITHIN THE CONTEXT OF UNION

Last week Joe and Lisa got married.

It was a sort of miracle, because neither of them expected they could thoroughly recover from their chronic conflicts and the recent acute trauma. As happy as they were, Lisa said she was sad that she could never trust him totally, and Joe was resentful that she had put him on endless probation. With this relational truth, they declared a psychological moratorium on the subject.

I said, "You are *both* on probation. Your marriage is not the end of the story. 'They got married and lived happily ever after' belongs to fantasy tales. In real life, it is 'They got married and worked even harder on their relationship.' The issues of trust, intimacy, conflicts about work versus home, desire versus fear of independence, a need for care and affection, valuing what the other may consider precious regardless of how silly it may seem to the other, will continue for all of your lives."

The setting of Jesus' first miracle—his transmuting water into wine—is a wedding ceremony in Cana. "All marriages take place at Cana," says a faithful Thomas Moore. Therefore all marriages are miracles.

At the unhappy end of the spectrum, others join Montaigne, who says, "The land of marriage has this peculiarity, that strangers are desirous of inhabiting it, whilst its natural inhabitants would willingly be banished thence." But it isn't the marriage that causes the dissatisfaction, it's the problems of the people involved in the relationship.

Marion Solomon, in her book on the power of positive dependency in intimate relationships, identifies these disturbances under the rubrics of defensive dependency, anxious attachment, boundary busting, fragile connection, and defensive distancing. An even greater poison in relationships is the issue of mistrust, earned or not. An old Sufi parable, "The Ancient Coffer," as told in Moore, is a case in point:

> *A very respected man named Nuri Bey had married a much younger woman. A faithful servant reported to him that the wife was behaving suspiciously—sitting alone guarding an old wooden trunk that was big enough to contain a body (i.e., another man). When he asked her to unlock the large chest, she refused to do so because it would mean acceptance of his mistrust. Instead she handed him the key to do so himself. After pondering the situation, Nuri Bey and his servants carried the unopened coffer far away and buried it.*

What was buried in that cold and lonely place was the soul of their marriage.

Most marriages start with some healthy ambivalence but also with good intentions. Two people faithfully enter an arrangement seeking many unspoken, if not unrecognized, fulfillments. They may end up with blissful epiphanies or bitter struggles. If an individual is expecting the partner to actualize his or her potential, that individual will frequently find that the partner falls short of that expectation, especially if the other is suffering from the same illusion. It is probably our idealization of relationships that causes marriage to be so vulnerable. One has to establish a healthy balance. If couples did not expect marriage to be their ultimate source of satisfaction, they would not be so susceptible to its disappointments. However, if their expectations are too low, even the marital relationships of people who relate well will take second place to work (mostly in men), children (mostly in women), or some other primary agenda.

Marriage at its best puts couples in a confusing dilemma: the attempt to have a union with someone else while maintaining an independent sense of self. Ambrose Bierce's *Devil's Dictionary* defines marriage as "the state or condition of community consisting of a master, a mistress, two slaves, making in all, two." The more the individual is undifferentiated, the greater the conflict with the partner. Marriage is a fertile ground for individuation as well as for union, but first one must be differentiated, just as a prisoner who wishes to help free his imprisoned companions must first break out of his own chains. Marriage requires attachment and individuation simultaneously, rather than sequentially, as it occurs in our early developmental years.

PREDICTOR OF LASTING MARRIAGE: GENERIC ALTRUISM AND SPECIFIC SELFISHNESS

It is overstated (but there is some truth to it) that in choosing a partner man tends to settle for physical beauty, and woman for a good provider, even though both seek many other qualities (intelligence, sense of humor, health, sensuality, good genes) as well. It is interesting that none of these qualities determines either the stability or the durability of a marriage. Obviously, no one enters a marriage with an expectation that it will not last. The conjugal vow "till death do us part" is a genuine belief at the time it is made, though heavily tainted with the excitements of sex and novelty. Therefore, mundane conflicts in the early stages of marriage are easily solved in bed. Sex becomes the "peace ground" for the couple.

Sex is also a battleground upon which many nonsexual skirmishes are fought. Because sexual intimacy invariably exposes one's vulnerabilities, it triggers some of the most primal fears and longings. Sexual contact may be experienced as an emotionally distant one-person affair or a blissful merging. Some individuals may feel unsafe in the sexual encounter—enslaved, engulfed, or disintegrated—while others may experience the reverse—comfort, intimacy, affection, passion, and exaltation. Sexual behavior is just another manifestation of the individual's maturational level.

Sex, beauty, and wealth are only transitory binders. By contrast, being generous to strangers, surviving each other's provocation, and honoring what is precious to the other are potentially permanent binders. I'll discuss generosity to strangers in the "Believing in Unity" chapter. Let's look at the other two potentially permanent binders now.

The Israeli biologist Amotz Zahavi believes that some otherwise mysterious conflicts might be explained by the mechanism of "testing of the bond." By provoking the partner, he contends, one may assess his or her willingness to continue to deliver the "goods of marriage" in the face of future difficulties. A basic question, of course, is whether all lovers (in different species) have spats to test each other. Zahavi answers by providing examples from courting birds. Female cardinals, says he, peck and chase wooing males and allow mating only after long persecution of their suitors. Their subsequent bond lasts for many seasons.

I think Joe and Lisa pecked and chased each other enough that their relation will likely survive future tests. But their individual growth *within* the marriage must continue. They will need continually to learn to protect each other's solitude and privacy, not to blame, to tolerate life triangulations and, last but not least, to cherish each other's peculiarities, no matter how foolish they may sound.

Honoring what is precious to the spouse is best portrayed in an African tale, as told by Harold Kushner, of a sky maiden:

> *A sky maiden married to an earthling caught her husband opening the huge locked box that belonged to her. He was more puzzled than guilty about this indiscreet act because he had discovered that the box was empty. When she angrily began to leave, he was perplexed and asked her what was so objectionable about peeking into an empty box. To his surprise she replied, "I'm not leaving you for the reason you think—it's not because you opened the box. Rather, it's because you called it empty. To me, it wasn't empty; it was full of sky and the aromas of my home. I can't be your wife if what is so precious to me is emptiness to you."*

THERE IS NO STAND-IN FOR A SOUL MATE

> *The Soul selects her own Society—Then—*
> *shuts the Door—*
> *To her divine Majority—*
> *Present no more.*

—Emily Dickinson

Not only are Lisa and Joe now husband and wife but they have become soul friends. They call each other lovingly by their soul names; he is Hippo and she is Piglet. "Soul mateness," more than emotional intimacy, grows with crises and adversities. Although it occasionally occurs in an initial encounter, soul matedness is developed over time. A soul mate is not found but cultivated. Soul mateness is not like love at first sight but more like W. W. Benjamin's "love at last sight." "From love of man one occasionally embraces someone in random," says Nietzsche. But one must remain in that embrace for a long time in order for that person to evolve to a soul mate. There is no microwave equivalent to it.

The Catholic Scholar John O'Donohue's recent exploration of our yearning to belong calls such soul friendships "eternal echoes." The soul relationship is a bond so special that neither space nor time could destroy it. It arouses an echo that resonates in the hearts of the friends forever, so that they experience a profound and intimate belonging with each other. Such a soulful relation offers a place to capture and hold all the longings of the human heart.

The sexual relation between soul mates is rarely a passionate one, although it might have started as such. When people talk about soul mates, we do not ask what they mean. We somehow understand, even though we ourselves might never have had such a relationship. We intuitively know that profound connection, that effortless communion. This precious intimacy crosses all boundaries of sex, age, and culture. It has all the elements of other intimate relationships, such as friends, lovers, or siblings, but is also quite distinct from them.

One can't will soul mateness as one may friendships, marriages, and work partnerships. One can only position oneself by being soulful. The soul mate will appear. The soulless person, in reaching for a soul mate, finds only himself again. He puts on a mask of soul but remains ego within. Such people may achieve important positions, accumulate great wealth, marry and have children, but they will always feel alone, and will make others feel even more so.

Mysteriously enough, even the most soulful of us rarely gets more than one chance in life to encounter a soul mate, because this relationship requires a sexual partner who is also a soulful person. Very few are graced with multiple opportunities. Do Joe and Lisa really value what they have? They have learned to accept what is precious to each other and definitely survived a number of provocation tests. I wonder now whether they'll remain embraced long enough to cultivate their souls. Somehow, human beings don't fully appreciate the preciousness of the gift of having a soul mate until we lose it. Then we begin our long and painful odyssey to find a replacement. Alas, there are no stand-ins for soul mates.

THE LOVE OF WORK

ALCHEMY: TRANSMUTING ORDINARY
WORK INTO SOUL

Underneath the tapestry, there is a mesh of
various rough threads.

—John O'Donohue

Glenn, a fifty-two-year-old divorced insurance agent had
been complaining about always being tired. He consulted
many internists, endocrinologists, and other specialists. They
found nothing physically wrong with him. All his tests were
normal. There was no hypothyroidism, no anemia, no low
blood pressure, no chronic infection, no precursor of malignant disease, and no deficiencies in vitamins or minerals. He
had a balanced diet and slept well enough. His testosterone
and other hormones were within normal ranges. One doctor
gave him antihistamines. Of all things, Glenn reported having allergic reactions to them! When another doctor sug-
gested an antidepressant, he refused. Finally a doctor gave
him the diagnosis chronic fatigue syndrome and sent him
away. (Physicians can be quite reductionistic: "Tell us what is
bothering you and we'll give it a name."

Glenn went to see a psychotherapist for a few months and found the process "tiring." The therapist thought he was depressed, tried to relate the onset of his symptoms to his divorce (three years ago), to his recent job change (seven months ago), and to his only daughter's marriage and moving out of the state (a year ago). But it seemed that Glenn had been "fatigued" for all his adult life. The cause and effect, in fact, were reversed. His wife finally left him because he was always tired, complained all the time about his work, got fired a few times, and changed jobs frequently, putting the family in financial jeopardy. She also didn't like that he would buy new cars, TVs, and stereos, take long vacations, and go to fancy restaurants with borrowed money. He explained that he had to feed his "inner child." In reality, he was suffering from an adult developmental arrest, reducing him to psychological inertia. For Glenn, even instant gratification wasn't fast enough.

Borrowing from the words displayed on the banner in front of Ficino's Florentine academy, we all seem to have adopted his Epicurean motto—Pleasure in the Present—without studying what the philosopher really meant. So we eat as much as we want, pursue our sexual interests, seek excitement all the time, spend money, possess things, and expand our leisure time. We even take his advice literally: "Let your meditation walk no further than pleasure, and even a little behind." This may seem an utterly hedonistic philosophy until we find out how Epicurus spent his life. For him pleasure was eating very little, and then only vegetables, spending his time in gardening, reading books, and being with friends.

Happiness doesn't mean gratification of all the senses, or constant and frenzied pursuit of excitement. We overvalue leisure time, and some people even try to figure out ways to rest during working hours. They keep complaining about their work and lack of sufficient time for relaxation. Yet if they allow themselves even greater leisure time, they experience deeper unhappiness. This is because the problem is not with the insufficiency of leisure time but with the concept of leisure itself. The fact is that leisure is enjoyable only if it follows work. A person who is genuinely engaged in his work is not preoccupied with whether he is happy or not.

Freud was once asked what he thought a happy, normal person should be able to do well. The questioner no doubt expected a complex and profound answer. Instead Freud's response was perhaps deceptively simple; he said, *"Arbeiten und Lieben"* ("to work and to love"). And if you love your work, the Sufis would go one step further and say, that is your faith. Dip your bread in your sweat, says another. Work is *liber mundi,* "book of the world," say Catholic monks, a life literacy, expressing the monks' religious duties, which are closely intertwined with their daily chores. Both activities are paths to divinity, provided they are carried out with the same profound soulfulness. Although contemporary secular work is a far cry from early monastic chores, it could be equally sacred if we could accept and deliver it with love and devotion. St. Thérèse of Lisieux, a nineteenth-century Carmelite nun, believed that God could be served best through small acts, thus advocating that care, compassion, and joy be brought to the little, everyday tasks of life.

Glenn had many jobs over the years. He was proud of being "multi-untalented and never playing the full deck." The fact that he was articulate, tall, and very well dressed meant he made a good impression and also could easily "rise above principles" and get a job, but he felt he was above doing ordinary work. He would sit at his desk, make a few business calls, and reluctantly write a couple of contracts, which he considered boring and empty chores. Self-addicted, as unhappy people tend to be, mostly he listened to the radio, watched TV, called 1–900 numbers, even got drunk on the job. He daydreamed daily about all kinds of silly things: how to become famous and very rich, and how to marry the actress Sharon Stone. While he was talking to a customer, he would simultaneously be elaborating on his fantasies. He made the worst of the best by his philosophy of "fake it, till you no longer make it; quit while you are behind." A large part of his mind was always elsewhere, because he could do all these jobs, he said, "with half a brain. And no one ever noticed." Of course, that wasn't all that true. Frequently he was found making mistakes because of his inattentiveness or lack of interest and was fired. As little as he seemed to work, by the end of the day he was totally exhausted. Unfortunately, neuroses don't crumble with fatigue only to unveil a counterfeit self. Marcel Marceau mimed the man who takes off one mask after another and finally discovers that he cannot tear the last one off. He is a sum of impersonations.

Every act of labor, no matter how ordinary and trivial it may seem, if attended with a depth of devotion and true imagination, will open a path for contemplation and holiness. But it must be true and real. The grandiose, unrealistic, and capricious kinds of imaginings that Glenn cultivates are quite different from devotional and simple thoughts and reflections, which do not spin into aimless and groundless fantasies. Willigis Jager's *Search for the Meaning of Life* portrays a man's grasping his "authenticity" as he goes deeper and deeper into his soul.

A man chopped underbrush at the edge of the forest, sold it, and lived on the modest profits. One day a hermit came out of the forest and advised him: "Go deeper into the forest!" The man went deeper into the forest and found wonderful trees, which he sold as timber. He became rich, but he suddenly recalled the advice of the hermit: "Go deeper into the forest!" And so he went deeper into the forest and found a silver mine. He worked it and became still more wealthy, but again the hermit's words occurred to him: "Go deeper into the forest!" Silver in hand, he walked on and on. Suddenly, at dawn, he found himself again at the edge of the forest. So he took his axe and chopped the underbrush and sold it to his fellows.

The soul is in simplicity, in the details of everyday chores, whether chopping wood, cleaning house or cooking a meal, washing dishes, typing, driving a bus, or just getting up and going to work. In his *Jewish Meditation,* Aryeh Kaplan shows how the simple task of dishwashing can be a transformation of the ordinary to soulfulness:

You are concentrating on the act of washing, clearing the mind of all other thoughts. Any other thought that enters the mind is gently pushed aside, so that the task at hand totally fills the mind. You are totally aware of the act you are doing. When a person develops such an awareness, then even the most mundane act can become an intimate experience of the Divine.

In our daily work, we are in that process of creativity, as an extension of God. We are created and we create. And that requires working and competence. As Mary McDermott Shideler puts it in her book *Spirituality,*

*For example, our answer to "What is the meaning of life?" will
not solve the question of which type and size of nail to use in lay-
ing a floor, how to adjust a cake recipe for high altitudes, or what
fingering is right for playing a particular musical phrase. No spiritual intention or achievement can compensate for technical
incompetence.*

Soulfulness is relevant to every aspect of the real world, from
the most widely general to the most minutely detailed, from the
loftiest to the most mundane, from games to skilled labor, artis-
tic endeavors, the raising of children, scientific investigations,
or any other domain. The extent to which we are aware of the
relevance of soulfulness will depend upon both our competence
and our willingness to make a commitment.

Different domains all have their own procedures and stan-
dards. That is, even if we play a game, we play by its rules.
And even though our attitude toward our opponent or the
game itself may be influenced by our general value system,
the actual moves we make in play reflect our knowledge of
the game's specific rules and strategies, and our commitments to the game at hand. Our failures in life are related not
necessarily to assumed handicaps or a lack of value systems
but to our *real* handicaps: the lack of full commitment to a
specific task. Beethoven wrote the timeless and sweeping
melodic "Ode to Joy" when he was totally deaf.

Executing insurance forms could have been fulfilling,
rewarding, and enlightening if Glenn had paid attention to
the meaning of his activity: brokering a serious contract
between two parties who trusted him to be fair, just, and
true. That is no doubt why the Zen master Shunryu Suzuki
(Suzuki Roshi) tells us that there is no such thing as an
enlightened person, just enlightened activity.

Enlightened activities are not only in the rituals of the temple but in the hard work of ordinary tasks. Rituals of the church and the faithful acts of the worshiper also need to be transported to the commonplace (*liturgy* means "the labor of laity"). Life that pivots around the temple remains as an example of the fullest divine intent. Nevertheless, the intention is not to differentiate between the sacred and the secular but to bring a reverence to everyday living. Whether the activity is in medicine or engineering or secretarial work or making furniture, we can bring to it soulful rituals, reminding us of the potential sacredness of *all* activities.

The ancient Greeks knew that the gods presided over every kind of work. For example, Hephaestus was the god of jewelry making. Japanese Buddhists still celebrate "needle memorial day" every February 8, a day on which the activity of sewing is honored.

It is not that some activities are soulful and others are not; it is about finding your own soulful activity. Wendell Johnson, in his *People in Quandaries,* tells the story of a man who played the bass violin, but in his own way.

> *The man's instrument had only one string, and he always kept his finger in the same place while he bowed that single string. He repeatedly played this way daily until his wife became completely exasperated. "Jack," she reprimanded, "why don't you play the bass violin the way other people do? Haven't you noticed that they have many strings on their bass violins, and that they keep moving their fingers up and down as they play their instrument?" "Of course they do," agreed her husband, then went on bowing. "The reason is that they're looking for the place. But, I've found it!"*

Weaving sacredness into daily life is the ultimate labor of the laity. One cannot fabricate such a soulful life only from within; it has to engage the world. The soul is not contained in us. Only some elements of the soul belong to the individual; the rest are out there in the world. When what seem to be ordinary sentiments, thoughts, feelings, and sensations of the inner life are mixed with what seem to be ordinary chores or things of the outer life, they are transmuted into the soul.

THERE ARE FINGERPRINTS
OF GOD ON EVERY "THING"

I must, before I die, find some way to say the essential thing that is in me, that I have never said yet—a thing that is not love or hate or pity or scorn, but the very breath of life, fierce and coming from far away, bringing into human life the vastness and fearful passionless force of non-human things.

—Bertrand Russell

During the past few weeks, Glenn had been home being treated for double pneumonia, which followed the ordinary flu. First no one, including the doctors, believed he was really sick until his illness got so bad that he was confined to bed. I went to visit him a few times. It was quite an experience.

Not only did Glenn possess many things that he didn't need but he also didn't take care of them. He'd neglect the maintenance of the car, his TV was always malfunctioning, the stereo system became mono, and when a tape was stuck in the VCR, he just left it there. He replaced whatever needed fixing and didn't even bother to throw away broken things, just put them in his garage. He had more than a dozen cameras, some working, some not. The place was chaotic and unpassable. Things were piled on top of one another. His adult daughter, who lived in Seattle, had been urging him to have a garage sale for years. Instead, he was still going to other people's garage sales and coming back with old lawn mowers, fans, calculators, and other objects, whether he needed them or not. There were four cars in his driveway in various states of disrepair. The windows of the house were so grimy, light could hardly get in. Dirt had accumulated on every object. I sank into one of his sofas, and a wave of dust engulfed me. There were dozens of letters and cards from his daughter on top of the desk, almost buried with other randomly thrown objects. Glenn, after seeing my reaction, sheepishly announced, "I guess I'm just lazy."

For centuries, both Western and Eastern religions have tried to convey to us the sacredness of all beings, including inanimate things. Christians, for instance, hold everyday objects in high regard as vessels with which they can serve God, and Jewish mystics have taught that every creation contains sparks of the divine. Hindus are known to take great pleasure in ordinary things, which are viewed as manifestations of Brahma, while Sufi poets are able to find the fingerprints of the Beloved on everything. Despite this broad and holy tradition of all religions, many of us still have a hard time honoring and caring for things. Like Glenn, many of us have too many possessions. We value them little, and treat them shabbily. Our materialism lacks depth.

This century is preoccupied with the accumulation of things. Every century has had similar preoccupations, except that they did not have as many choices. Industrial society provided refrigerators, radios, televisions, videocassette recorders, and cars to almost every household. There is nothing inherently wrong with having possessions. It is only when consumption becomes a life philosophy that it undermines seeking higher meaning in life. The philosophy of consumption results in a sense of futility and internal unworthiness.

Paul Nystrom, an early student of modern marketing, portrays the industrial civilization as giving rise to a philosophy of futility, a pervasive fatigue, a disappointment with achievements. It finds an outlet in changing everything into the more superficial things of life, in which fads reign. The tired and unappreciated laborer, instead of changing the conditions of work, and often defeated in his or her attempts to do so, seeks an easier route: renewal in temporarily brightening the immediate surroundings with new goods.

Ironically, and predictably, the propaganda of consumption turns even alienation into a commodity. In short, it may address itself to the spiritual desolation of modern life but finds itself proposing consumption as the cure. It sings the negation of immortality and the futility of everything holy. The Industrial Workers of the World's (IWW) union chant is a case in point:

> *Work and pray,*
> *Live on hay!*
> *You'll get pie,*
> *In the sky,*
> *When you die—*
> *It's a lie.*

THE HAPPINESS IS SUBTRACTION

When our functional mind applies its technological efficiency and mathematical orderliness to emotional states, it breaks down happiness into its presumed components and measures these components by quantifiable elements: a beautiful dress, a marriage, a promotion, a car, a vacation, lots of money, and the like; multiplies those things with an intensity of addiction; and ends up darkening the world with clutter to the point that no light of life can get in.

No addition ever brings contentment, never mind happiness. As Gary Zukav says in *The Seat of the Soul,* "An addiction cannot be satisfied by its object." You hear people saying, "I have everything I wanted: health, money, family, science, et cetera. Why am I not happy?" The reason is that the wish to acquire possessions and power works against the achievement of happiness. Only if you wish for what you already have will you be closer to happiness. In an experiment at the State University of New York at Buffalo, subjects were asked to complete the sentence "I'm glad I'm not a . . ." After five repetitions of this exercise, the subjects experienced a distinct elevation in their feelings of life satisfaction. Another group of subjects were asked by the experimenters to complete the sentence "I wish I were a . . ." This time the experiment left the subjects feeling more dissatisfied with their lives. Possessions and achievements may register only on the scale of addition. Happiness, however, is measured on the scale of subtraction. The love of God is the emptying of the house so that light can get in. Did Jesus say, when hallowed you'll be full?

ATTACHMENT TO BEINGS REQUIRES
DETACHMENT FROM THINGS

In my profession, as in the roofing business, the leak is rarely where the drip is. Glenn's self-accusation of laziness was a kind of pleading guilty to a lesser charge. He eventually confessed to a greater one: He wasn't sure whether he cared about anything at all but, more to the point, he cared even less about people. "I really have no friends. I never loved my wife. I guess I kind of care about my daughter. She doesn't think so because I don't write to her."

He was beginning to enjoy his self-recognition: "I do get bored with people. Whenever life gets bad I go collecting. It is not 'I shop therefore I am.' No, it's worse than that. 'The things are me!' I know it is wrong, I am kind of embarrassed by that, but I seem to be a 'thing person' not a 'people person.' Relationships don't do it for me. I feel good and safe and comfortable when I can own things and more things. I know it is crazy."

If one's selfhood and self-worth are closely associated with possessions, one sees a frantic search for acquisition, as desire is trapped within the unsatisfied self—a sort of psychological infection. As a consequence, the soul's needs can at best become expressed in a host of compromises, in which spiritual growth is stunted.

Unfortunately, as the philosopher Henri Bergson says, the human intellect feels at home among inanimate objects, especially in a culture of action, industry, and tools. The battle for the soul has to be not buttressed by objects but arrived at by objectlessness.

Modern culture is deeply lonely. This is partly because we are attached to things and detached from people. There is no satiety in possessing things, because they do not fill the psychological vacuum. In fact, the more one acquires things, the deeper the hole gets, to such a degree that no "things" can fill it. John of the Cross proposes:

> *To come to possess all*
> *Desire the possession of nothing.*

To arrive at being all
Desire to be nothing.
To come to the knowledge of all
Desire the knowledge of nothing. . . .
To come to be what you are not
You must go by a way in which you are not.

Of course, one need not go to such extremes to have a soulful life. There is a balance. Only excessive attachment to and desire for things interfere with the devotion that is required for intimate relationships and a soulful existence.

As much as a relative detachment from things is needed to enrich the soul, any detachment from intimates would impoverish it. From infancy until death, we draw our strength from our relations and, in return, give strength to them. From youth to old age—from rocking horse to rocking chair—friendship is what keeps teaching us about being human, writes the cultural observer Letty Cottin Pogrebin. The intimate sharing of ideas and ideals, empathic support that is deeply felt and caring, enduring admiration and fidelity reach the shores of our soul. From childhood pals to adult mentors and friends, special individuals draw out the best that is in us (and we in them), as together we and they are witnesses to our self-discoveries and soulful unfolding.

CARVING THE BACK OF A MASTERPIECE

Glenn came to a session slightly inebriated and began to lecture me. "Doc, you must be an anal character. Look at this office, everything is in perfect order, not a thing is out of place. All items are well-proportioned and are at 90- to 180-degree angles to each other. The floor is so clean you can eat from it. I am sure your kitchen and your bedroom are all the same way. Doc, what is this all about? Who cares? Listen, I don't make my bed every morning. Why? Because I'll be getting into it the same night and messing it up again. So why make it?" Then he got up and moved one of the prints that was a little crooked on the wall and sat down again with a mischievous smile.

The things I keep around me are all soul makers. I take care of them because they are all sacred things. When they are clean and balanced, and my space is uncluttered, they are transformative. I work better when these things are taken care of. I spend many hours in my office. Usually my thoughts, feelings, and ideas ferment here.

The Persian mystic Rūmi uses the image of a winery and the process of fermentation as a metaphor for soulmaking. Fermentation—a chemical change with effervescence—is one of the earliest symbols for transformation. After all, from the simple and natural process of fermenting the juice of grapes comes extraordinary results.

Similarly, the soul ferments in its environment and gets its nurturance not simply from its "food" per se but from the process of feeding. Even inexpensive grapes ferment to wine. All things and activities of ordinary life are potential sources for such sacred nurturing and fermenting of the soul. The objects, expensive or inexpensive, are the food of our environment, and cleaning them is the feeding process. Together they transform the place, whether home or office, into soulmaking.

Soulful life is not an abstract concept. It is woven into the vernacular. Its ingredients are the stuff of daily living, personal and communal. The living and eternal truth is expressed in work only insofar as that work is true in itself.

No other feedback, reward, or recognition is required. It is all done for God's eyes only, as was the work of the anonymous artisans in medieval times, who would carve the back of a work of art, believing that though no human eyes would see it, God's eyes would.

STRIPPING DOWN TO THE BARE SOUL

Glenn was clever, facile, confrontative, and dismissive. He made fun of any concept that wasn't visible, tangible, audible, or edible. He considered the soul, the spirit, as the production of soft minds, twelve steps to "robotville." Most people— wife, friends, doctors—gave up on him because they mistook his façade for his core. But to get beyond such an entrenched self-presentation requires faith in every person's potential for soulmaking.

Soulmaking is patiently cultivating one's soul. It is not that one either has a fully formed soul or doesn't. The soul is always in a state of ascension. You should not be discouraged if you don't experience the soul's full presence. The first step is to find out the real nature of your self—your simple, rough form— and become transparent to yourself. For that you need to free yourself from all other forms that you may have accumulated in your adult life. Donna Schaper, a minister of the United Church of Christ, has a perfect metaphor for such self-stripping as she refinishes a chair. She calls it "stripping down."

The first thing people do when restoring old chairs is strip—strip right down to the bare wood. They strip away all the years of grime, the garish coats of paint piled one on top of the other. They get rid of all the junk that's been tacked on through the years and try to find the solid, simple thing that's underneath.

Never mind the stripping down. Glenn wouldn't even take off his steel overcoat. Even his "psychological confessions," such as not caring about people or being lazy, had a rationalizing, if not a bragging quality.

Glenn thought he had figured out the world. "Feelings interfere with the mind, Doc," he said. "I know what I am all about, my thinking is crystal clear. Though you may doubt, I don't."

If there is anything that *doesn't* have an intrinsic status, it is thinking. The philosopher Descartes, by his conclusion *Cogito, ergo sum* (I think, therefore I am), unintentionally provided intellectual defenses for people like Glenn, who overvalue their minds. The soul reverses Descartes's articulation, because it is mysterious, confounding, and often contrary. It defies the self-validation of logic. James Hillman says that only God knows our real name, and he describes how we may come close to finding what that is, not by cognitive exercises but by way of self-transparency. Once the soul is wholly revealed, one is just what one is. That transparency will serve as a prism, and all the rays of divinity will emanate from within. Artists are endowed with maximum transparency. Their work intensifies emotions, heightens the sense of existence, and invites contemplation. One need not be a fine artist. Woodworking, gardening, writing letters, weaving, or knitting could serve as a prism.

Letter writing is, in fact, a perfect example of such a prism. I suspect that is why Glenn wouldn't reply to his daughter's letters and risk self-exposure. Writing is a self-reflective conversation. In actual conversation, immediate feedback from the listener shapes not only the content of the talk but also the speakers. One never is oneself in a dialogue. Occasionally, we are surprised by the unintended results of our conversation with someone. In contrast, writing letters is a deliberate monologue, the main audience being the writer—him or herself. Letter writing is a structured form of self-contemplation. Even a few minimal sentences can easily reflect one's inner light. In fact, just a simple pausing or a period of reflective nondoing could serve as the prism. "God is the minimum as well as the maximum," said Nicholas of Cusa.

I WORK, THEREFORE I AM

Glenn never liked to work, never mind work very hard. He was always told that he was coasting and trying to get away with the minimum effort possible. He was fired from his last job because he left exactly at 5:00 P.M. and did not close an important deal that day. What he really wanted was to get some income through the workers' compensation fund because of his chronic fatigue syndrome, or any disease for that matter.

Glenn recited a long litany against doctors, how they were interested only in money. They wouldn't give a damn if he lived or died. He wasn't getting any better, and they weren't returning his calls, although they kept sending their bills. He got one call from the doctor's office just to remind him that his payment was overdue. Meanwhile, he was always renegotiating my fee—downward, of course—and still not paying it. He had a sense of humor about it, though. Once he began the session by saying, "Here I am again, Doctor." Noticing that I didn't get the joke, he took special pleasure in telling me about Groucho Marx. He saw a sign in front of a doctor's office which read: "First visit 10 cents, and thereafter 5 cents." He walked in and said, "Here I am again, Doctor."

There is a similar story about a Sufi, Nasreddin, who goes to a teacher for music lessons. "How much do the lessons cost?" he asks. "Fifteen dollars for the first lesson, ten dollars each after that," says the teacher. "Fine," Nasreddin replies. "I'll begin with lesson number two."

In spite of a thousand years between them, and an enormous cultural gap, these two stories have two things in common: our tendency to want to begin with the second visit or lesson and the expectation of a quick result.

The soulful take the first, the last, and all lessons with enthusiasm, patience, and steadfastness—neither success nor failure occurs overnight and makes work real, no matter how small or big, pleasant or painful, clean or dirty the job. Bees get honey from every flower. When you do something, says Shunryu Suzuki in *Zen Mind, Beginner's Mind,*

you should do it with your whole body and mind; you should be concentrated on what you do. You should do it completely, like a good bonfire. You should not be a smoky fire.

Such an individual works with enthusiasm, does what has to be done, again and again, and transforms her or himself into the native element of common harmony. In her poem "To Be of Use," Marge Piercy portrays this process:

The people I love the best
jump into work head first
without dallying in the shallows
and swim off with sure strokes almost out of sight.
They seem to become natives of that element.
I love people who harness themselves, an ox to a heavy cart,
who pull like water buffalo, with massive patience,

who strain in the mud and the muck to move things forward,
who do what has to be done, again and again.

And it isn't even that difficult. The winds of grace are always blowing; all you have to do is raise the sail, but enthusiastically. *Enthusiasm* means "the God within"—to be one with God's energy—and its sparks come from the *Ruach Elohim,* the spirit of God. In the Kabbala, God channeled a ray of light through mystic vessels. Some of them shattered. The world became broken. And fallen sparks of the eternal dissolved in every aspect of our mundane existence. Through good works, prayer, and mystical contemplation, man raised the sparks back to God and repaired the world.

KARMIC DEBTS: THE LOVE THAT GOES OUT TO WORK COMES BACK AS LOVE OF SELF

I asked Glenn whether he liked any job that he has had in his life. He replied, "Well, I hated my first job, which was newspaper delivery; I must have been about twelve. Rain and shine I had to get on my bicycle to go around the neighborhood and throw the papers on people's lawns. Actually some expected me to put them in their mailboxes. How pathetic! They all had these silly dogs who would chase me. I'd hit them with their owners' newspaper until between me and the dogs snapping at it, the newspaper would be all shredded."

"Did you like any of your neighbors?" I inquired.

"I never knew who they were, with few exceptions. They lived close to our house. There was this fat couple who demanded that I bring the paper all the way to their door because they were so damn lazy, and then there was an Italian widow who gave me garlic-smelling cookies. No, I didn't like the neighbors or my employers; in fact, I hated them all. Bosses in the insurance business are the worst. They want to extract every penny from the customer, and every drop of blood from the employees. How could you like such people? In between, I was assistant coach, maître d', salesman, manager. For a while I co-owned a car dealership, which went bankrupt thanks to my crooked partner. All those places were alike. You are supposed to do all that ordinary work without any merit and meaning. If you don't succeed you are running above average." In fact, one must extract meaning even from seemingly meaningless activities.

The magical process of transmuting ordinary materials into something of true merit requires commitment and love of one's work; meaning emerges as a by-product of such an engagement. The primary satisfaction is in finding in one's work that which corresponds to one's inner self and not seeking exclusively secondary gains, such as prestige, money, and other trappings. These secondary satisfactions take on greater significance if one's work no longer reflects one's real self but is used to project a false self. Modern life, by distancing the worker from the product, unfortunately makes it harder for the individual to identify with the outcome and to love it, never mind to assimilate with one's work in an alchemical fashion. But, it is worth trying, even under such adverse conditions, because, in Thomas Moore's words, "the love that goes out into our work comes back as love of self." Such self-love is not self-adoration, nor is it self-indulgence; it is a reflection of one's self in one's work.

The extraordinary filmmaker Jean Renoir is a perfect example of this love of work. He says, "For, after all, I have been happy. I have made the films I wanted to make, I have made them with people who were more than my collaborators; they were my accomplices. This, I believe, is one recipe for happiness: To work with people you love and who love you." That was the case even though, at times, he must have been discouraged by the limited financial value of his work.

We see the signatures of all souls in the works of those who are committed. Old farmers from the small British village of Akenfield could look at a field where several men had plowed and tell you the name of the man who had done each furrow because each furrow so reflected the character of that particular plowman. In Indian markets in South America where they sell rope, you can tell who made each and every piece. There is a great difference between such innate character and an artificial or conscious attempt at a "personal" statement, or insincere work for mercenary motives. Indeed, when those farmers in Akenfield were asked why they took such care to make furrows so precise (especially since the precision would not yield more beans), they replied simply that it was their work and they did it as best they could. It did not merely belong to them, it *was* them. It was the very signature of the person, the work of life.

The signature of work matures with full commitment of energy and singular intention. This kind of intention means holding your attention on the desired outcome with such unbending purpose that you refuse to allow obstacles to dissipate its focus. There is a total and complete exclusion of all resistant forces from your consciousness. You are able to maintain an unshakable serenity while being committed to your goal with intense passion.

As the old saying goes, "The sun's rays fall everywhere uniformly, but only where they are focused through a magnifying glass can they set dry grass on fire." In all his works, simple or complicated, Glenn's signature was missing, at times quite literally. His noncommitted way of working was a depressant, even though he thought that by lack of full engagement he was protecting himself from depressing drudgery. In fact, the contrary is true. Totally engaged work is an effective *anti*depressant. Robert Burton, in his opening address to the reader of *The Anatomy of Melancholy,* says, "I write of melancholy, being busy to avoid melancholy. There is no greater cause of melancholy than idleness, no better cure than business. When you have unlimited time with yourself, the danger is that you will tear yourself apart."

Most ordinary people lift heavy loads at work—literally or figuratively. But the principle remains the same, that loving one's work makes even the most difficult labor rewarding. Similarly, in *The Art of Selfishness* (and by association, the art of self*less*ness), David Seabury describes miners who dig for diamonds, shoveling tons of dirt to find the smallest chip. But the miners are not concentrating on the dirt. They are willing to do inordinate amounts of digging in order to find the tiniest jewel. In everyday living, however, we tend to forget this principle, especially when life seems to be more dirt than diamonds.

SHARING THE JOY AND THE BURDEN

Part of Glenn's reluctance to engage with his work was related to the fact that he never learned any task well, so he always felt inadequate to the job. Usually, he managed to limp along, and when things got tougher, that is, when his incompetence could no longer be hidden underneath his devil-may-care attitude, he quickly left. The failure had gone to his head. His arrogance didn't allow him to learn under the guidance of someone else, especially when the person was younger than himself. If he was going to succeed, he was going to do it alone. That is a common source of failure, as in this tale by David J. Wolpe:

> *A boy and his father were walking along a road when they came across a large stone. The boy said to his father, "Do you think if I use all my strength, I can move this rock?" His father answered, "If you use all your strength, I am sure you can do it." The boy began to push the rock. Exerting himself as much as he could, he pushed and pushed. The rock did not move. Discouraged, he said to his father, "You were wrong. I can't do it." His father placed his arm around the boy's shoulder and said, "No, son. You didn't use all your strength—you didn't ask me to help."*

WORK THEATER OF EVERYDAY LIFE

Glenn's maladaptive work pattern is a common example of the damaging of one's soul. There are two other groups whose work scenarios may look very adaptive, if not admirable, on the surface but are equally dispiriting to the individual, his co-workers, and his family members. One is the person who wants to have every role in the play, so to speak, including the director. He tries to do everything himself but doesn't share the power and responsibility with others and makes himself indispensable. The second type can play a role only if it is defined by others. He becomes a performer and forfeits his authentic calling.

People who tend to take over everything are more tiring than tired. Independent of their competence, they feel uncomfortable in delegating and micromanage every detail. They think that if they don't, either it will not be done or it will be done incorrectly. They have no confidence in others, regardless of their competency.

The one who is trying to do everything herself not only forfeits others' potential but also cannot really succeed. As the tasks expand, such a person eventually feels not only chronic exhaustion but also underappreciation. Even Moses couldn't escape the despair and irritation of having excessive responsibility: when the people of Israel began complaining out loud about having only manna (a kind of coriander seed) to eat, and accusing Moses of taking them out of Egypt, where they ate all the free fish, cucumbers, watermelons, leeks, onions, and garlic they wished, Moses went to the Lord and said: "Why have you brought me this trouble? . . . Am I their mother? . . . Where can I get meat for all these people? . . . I can't take care of all these people by myself. This is too much work for me."

The distribution of power and responsibility to one's team not only preserves the competent person's energy and well-being but also cultivates the competence of others, ultimately benefiting everyone. The one who has real power (personality, intelligence, judgment) will welcome all the help she needs even though doing so may seem to dilute her authority and significance. Ultimate authority and significance come not by holding on to the center of power and having others feel totally dispensable but by making oneself relatively dispensable.

The second group tends to confuse living with performance. How we want to be is not necessarily what is expected of us. If the conflict between the two resolves in favor of the latter, we end up performing for others—our parents, teachers, spouses, friends, ministers, even our children. The authentic self is so often compromised that eventually its spirit is broken and becomes unidentifiable or, worse, it becomes one with the performing self. Such invasive bureaucratization of the self uproots the soul to the point that one can no longer experience genuine emotions, except perhaps a vague unhappiness, which engenders futility of work, negates love, and promulgates a philosophy of nihilism.

WINNING BY LOSING

The Shah of Persia refused to be taken to the Derby Day, saying, "It is already known to me that one horse can run faster than another."

—William James

With each change of job and the repetition of the pattern of "reluctant warrior," Glenn was accumulating another failure. He was getting older, lonelier, more helpless, and his health—but not his arrogance—was declining. He knew neither how to strip down all those self-destructive layers of defenses and try to build a success on his failures nor how simply to come to terms with the bare reality of the failure and seek some sweetness in it.

Even successful men face a similar difficult task toward the last phase of their lives unless they learn to transcend the concept of winning. The story of the Shah of Persia that begins the section is an example of transcending the win-lose paradigm. The end of one's career, one's wealth, and one's good health in general hits men quite hard. The idea of retirement may be equivalent to castration, if not death, for men whose identity is built around work, especially if the work has been successful. Winning, which has been their driving force since their childhood games, naturally gains an overarching significance, independent of what is to be won or lost.

Old men appear older, lonelier, and more helpless than women. Power (and the self-assurance it brings), the very thing that men pursue, keeps slipping through their fingers. Traditionally, women have built enduring personal connections that help them survive losing scenarios. But if the winning is defined only by careers, wealth, and power at the expense of health, genuine intimacy, and loving engagements in daily life, this winning may be the ultimate losing.

Women bear and raise children, feed the family, clean house, do other chores, drive kids to school, games, or their friends' houses and pick them up, read them bedtime stories, and worry about their illnesses, their school, and their social lives, often while working outside the home. There is no way fully to appreciate the selflessness of these mothers, for they are invisible at the end product. They are the real carvers of the backs of masterpieces. Men have a great deal to learn from them, to find their calling, then work hard lovingly, and simultaneously build enduring intimate relationships that can make successes even out of failures. A verse from the Spanish poet Antonio Machado is eloquent on this point:

> *Last night, as I was sleeping,*
> *I dreamt—marvellous error!—*
> *that I had a beehive here inside my heart.*
> *And the golden bees were making white combs*
> *and sweet honey from my old failures.*

THE LOVE OF BELONGING

The tallest trees send down roots as they rise toward Light.

—James Hillman

THE SOUL NEEDS A FERTILE SOIL

Thelma is a thirty-nine-year-old single computer analyst who always felt mildly anxious and depressed because she had "no man in my life, and no real, real friends." She dismissed others simply as acquaintances. "Actually I wouldn't need friends if I had a boyfriend," she claimed. She liked her work, was appreciated and well rewarded financially. But that was it, and at the end of the day, she didn't want to go home. She'd stay and work a few extra hours after everyone else had left. When the cleaning crew would gently force her out, she'd walk around the city to delay getting home. She would try to skip dinner, since she had been attempting to lose twenty pounds, but would cave in to her impulse, buy a box of Entenmann's donuts from the local store, and eat half of it before she got to her place. Then she would throw the rest in the garbage can, only to retrieve it later that night.

All she needed, she would say, was a man in her life. Oth-

erwise, she loved the total freedom that came from not having any attachments. She described herself as being
"obsessed" with men but had not had much luck with them.
Although reasonably attractive, she had had only a few
boyfriends when she was younger. But lately her dates ended
up being one-orgasm stands: theirs. She had read all the
books about how to converse with men, followed the Knicks,
Yankees, and Rangers, learned the names of their players,
and studied the sexual and communication behavior of
"Martians." But she never had the chance to violate any one
of the "rules" in relating to men. Whether she called them or
not made no difference. *They* never called. She was beginning to worry that she'd never find a good husband. There
were those "nerds" (her word) in her life who were interested
in her, but, "Who would want them? Imagine having children with them, the genetic pool for ugly ducklings!" She
had strong feelings about men. She hated bald men, short
men, fat men, and guys wearing glasses.

She didn't know how other women meet men. Her therapist, with whom she felt like a steppatient, interpreted
Thelma's relations with men as "frenetic passivity," based on
"fear-fulfillment." The introductions from co-workers to
blind dates all proved to be disasters. After seeing the movie
You've Got Mail a few times, she got into a chat room of
interest, only to meet a Yugoslavian man who was looking
for a U.S. citizen to marry so that he could get a visa. She
abhorred the idea of meeting through the personal ads, but
on one of her most desperate evenings, she carefully selected
one from *New York* magazine's personals' section: "42 wsm,
prof., 5'9", blond, athletic seeks young, beautiful woman who
enjoys walks in the park, dinners by candlelight, movies and
emotional intimacy and more."

She couldn't sleep the night before their appointed time and place to meet. His apartment, 6:00 P.M. sharp. *He had to leave by 6:15?* When she rang the bell, her heart was beating so loudly she could hear it. A well-dressed man opened the door and said, "Yes?" She answered, "I'm Thelma." The man closed the door in her face. She stood there stunned for a few minutes. "Why would he do that? Am I that ugly?" she wondered. "And what kind of a person would do such a thing to another human being?" She was devastated. For two days she couldn't even function. First, she wanted to go back to the man's apartment and confront him. Then she thought about setting a fire in front of his door or spray-painting it. But that would not bring enough satisfaction. "An appropriate retaliation would be to kill him. This kind of man shouldn't be alive and be loose in the community," she decided. Fortunately, her rage gradually subsided, but her obsession with finding a man did not.

Thelma's "obsession" with men wasn't about sex; she had never had an orgasm with intercourse. "Actually," she said, "I prefer masturbation. It isn't their companionship either. To tell the truth, it is a major effort to converse with men. I much prefer women's company," she claimed. She just wanted to be married: "If man has one song to sing, women have two: husband and weight." She traced her obsession about men to breaking her "pathological" ties with her family two years ago when she moved to New York. In Thelma's house there was no physical sexual abuse, but there was chronic psychological abuse, which lowered her self-esteem. Her mother explicitly preferred her older sister. Her father spent all his free time with her younger brother. Deprived or rejected by both parents, she felt all alone. Thelma was told by her previous therapist to stay away from her family, because it was a "hothouse for neuroses," and that unless she broke away, she could never establish a family of her own. Furthermore, the therapist said her resistance to falling into a "transferential bond" with him was caused by her pathological preoccupation with her family. Though the therapist's attempt at this artificial induction of therapeutic illness didn't totally succeed, Thelma physically removed herself from her family, including her siblings, and made herself even lonelier and more disconnected. Psychologically, though, she was always preoccupied with them, especially her mother. She could not sever the negative bond, no matter what.

The parent-children unit is the supreme regulating principle of life. If one extends the same concept to the *parents* of the mother and father, that influence becomes even more powerful. What gives such a presence to the family is a deeply grounded and lasting intergenerational relationship that establishes internal security in its members. Cohesiveness, by connecting the roots of the past with the branches of the present, solidifies the family for the future. More extended families provide fertile ground for nourishing ties that protect their members against the anxiety of aloneness in the world. Cut flowers don't last long, and even the strongest tree can't survive once it is uprooted. The family that establishes deep and wide roots offers fertile ground to the soul.

If the natural ground of the immediate family is lacking certain good, nourishing raw materials, then the soul must branch out to blood relatives and to other long-standing relationships for history and a sense of belonging. Such childhood as well as adult relationships, maintained and nurtured, generate strong ties that give meaning to life. Our fondest stories are about the group activities that we were part of, whether in the army fighting a war or demonstrating against it, playing on a sports team or cheering for it, working on a campaign or for a cherished charity. These events were not necessarily poetic or mythic at the time of their occurrence, but by integrating their memories we give them a voice, an echo that reverberates with the myth of our own family in a larger sense of the word.

All these relationships to others in the community eventually are transmuted to our immediate family, which is the first and most enduring of our ties. We all need to feel connected to our original family, no matter how conflicted it may have been. The family is our initial anchoring point. The deeper the water, that is, the greater the stress, the deeper the anchor must go. We all have families, good or bad, happy or unhappy, functional or dysfunctional. In fact, such polarizations (as discussed at the individual level) may themselves be just myths, fictions that we are unable, or unwilling, to dispel. With the exception of the serious violations, like physical, emotional, or sexual abuse which generate time-release trauma for life, the garden variety of problems a family might face are fundamentally nourishing to its members, helping their growth and emotional enrichment, despite adversity or pain.

The secular experiences of a family, like religious ones, imprint on the individual's soul. They can be ordinary interactions, frequently full of conflicts and contentions, jealousy, envy, and competition and, at times, ugly and dirty. After all, the Bible's Book of Genesis reminds us that Adam was formed out of the dust of the earth. The individual as well as the family is part of the whole of nature, as natural as the mud of the earth. Any attempt to destroy the impurities of nature also removes the fertile soil. Therefore, any excessive "cleansing" of family behavior may make it more socially

acceptable but also sterilizes its soul. There are some therapists who, by their clinical reductionism, diagnose a family
and prescribe remedies to make their behavior more "normal." By not recognizing the formative mythology in the
family conflicts, however, they tend to jump too quickly to
figure out problems, and they are able to provide only superficial or antiseptic solutions. This approach is like pulling a
thread sticking out in a cloth, unraveling the texture that
holds together the individuals in the family, which is intricately interwoven to form a rich pattern. The therapist's role,
rather, should be to appreciate that richness and help the
individuals search deep in their stories to find the formative
myths in the family and connect them with the communal
archetypal family. The family that remains differentiated
from the myth of the archetypal family is lonely, confused,
and alienated. Its members experience themselves as aberra-
tions, disconnected from the past, the present, and the future.

GROWING DOWN: BECOMING BY BELONGING

In her growing up years, Thelma never felt that she totally
belonged to her family; for a long time she was sure she was
adopted. Her sense of alienation extended to school and her
neighborhood. The family moved frequently because of her
father's job, which didn't help. Her mother would find any
friend Thelma brought home strange, crazy, sick, or otherwise unacceptable, "not our kind of people." She discouraged
Thelma from going to parties and other gatherings. Thelma
felt awkward, if not foolish, in social situations anyway. "I
had nothing to say worth listening to, nothing to offer," she
said. She was curious about what other kids talked about
with a sense of urgency and laughter. Occasionally they

would glance at her. "Could they be talking about me, laughing at me?" she wondered. She still has remnants of those feelings. "Why don't other people ever approach me and initiate a conversation? No one invites me to any parties or asks me to visit their weekend houses. I overhear my co-workers talking: 'Are you getting a ride to the Hamptons or taking the jitney?'" Thelma went through life without maintaining friendships because they were not "intimate enough." At the age of thirty-eight, she had no one from her past even in her memory. Now she had no "crazy" family either. She belonged to no one and no place. No wonder she was chronically anxious and depressed.

Both psychologists and philosophers assert that one has to "be" before one can "belong." But being and belonging feed into each other. Being is not a static state; it is ever evolving; one acquires only degrees of being. In fact, it may be more accurate to refer to "becoming" rather than "being." Belonging becomes intricately woven into the process of one's becoming.

The infant is born into a world. The immediate world of that infant is the mother, from whom he or she cannot differentiate. Simply by belonging to its mother, the infant has its needs met. The mother's relationship to the infant isn't just that of a grown-up taking care of the helpless, although an element of this is always present; primarily it is a primitive, if mysterious, bond. We share that primitive mystery with the community of all animals. Among penguins, who seem to be incapable of hurting anything, a mother will harshly push away a lost baby penguin of another mother. That innate instinct to preserve her own is universal. By contrast, human beings, and even some animals, are capable of adopting and nurturing others' offspring. Such altruism flies in the face of

all genetic science and is explainable only by the mysterious-
ness of our belonging to each other at some fundamental
level of communion.

As an infant matures, a psychological birth occurs: the
child begins to differentiate from maternal belonging to
independent being; he or she starts relating to others: father,
siblings, relatives, grandparents, neighbors. At first the child
is passively loved and introduced into the community of the
family; all that is required of him is a minimum of reciprocation, like a little smile. By school age, though, he'll be
expected to seek and engage actively, to maintain member-
ship in the community. He must relate to teachers, class-
mates, and friends, participate in extracurricular activities, be
able to socialize and fully engage with other people. Some
older children, and even adults, will maintain that passive-
receptive attitude of younger years in relation to the community, always waiting to be recruited. But belonging is an
activity, and it requires time, energy, and commitment. As
the old saying goes, if you want to have friends, then be one.
Some individuals remain aloof, afraid of their limitations,
believing that their shortcomings might be discovered or
their foolishness exposed. But this stance leads ultimately to a
self-fulfilling prophecy: their rejection by others. This
assumption of a handicapped self implies the perfection of
others. In fact, we are all limited in our own ways.

Thelma's statement that she wouldn't really need friends
if she had a man in her life is a common defensive illusion
and a maladaptive one. Even good marriages cannot survive
in such isolation. We need friends and less intimate relationships as much as the most intimate ones, for they serve different degrees of belonging. Even if Thelma found a "perfect"
mate and had children, they would not bring what she is

yearning for. Research shows that while no amount of friendship is sufficient to compensate for the loss of close attachments and emotional intimacy, intimate personal relationships alone do *not* provide life with meaning. Robert S. Weiss studied couples who in the course of their marriage had moved away from the neighborhood in which they had settled. He found that intimate attachments to their spouses remained intact, but what distressed them was no longer feeling part of a larger group. These findings suggest that whether or not they are enjoying intimate relationships, human beings need something else—a sense of being part of a community that goes beyond the one constituted by immediate family and other intimate relationships.

The universe often feels too big for us, and we yearn for a secure nest, a contained belonging. This sense of belonging to something defined also protects us from the other side of the intimacy coin, the feeling of inner infinity that each of us secretly carries and that we may sometimes experience as a boundless abyss. When we belong to a community or group, we have a structured and bounded mooring to protect us from the amorphous threat of the infinite from without and within.

Thelma's choice of freedom from attachments, which was at least partly a conscious decision, created total isolation for her. As Peter L. Berger says in *A Far Glory,* making a deliberate choice condemns one to freedom that generates existential anxiety. Any reversible decision obtained by free choice doesn't stabilize the self. Even choosing one's religion doesn't help the anxiety, as one presumes it might. This is because choosing itself, even if the subject matter is faith, is a choice. Since it can be reversed, it can be destabilizing. The self cannot be a matter of decision.

Erich Fromm viewed the escape from freedom in his book of the same name, *Escape from Freedom,* as a remedy for existential anxiety and our "quest for community." The basic structure of the community imposed upon individuals provides a security of belonging without choice. In contrast to condemnation to freedom, in imposed community one is offered the salvation of restraint. Instead of the existential anxiety of freedom, one is provided with the peacefulness of communion.

Thelma believed that, for women, sex is primarily used for the purpose of bonding. Therefore, on her occasional dates she would sleep with the men in the hope of engaging them in a relationship. She took appropriate precautions so she wouldn't get pregnant. As desperate as she was for a man, she wasn't about to get married to anyone. Most women take sex more seriously than do men, and they have a practical reason for this seriousness—they bear the greater consequences.

Besides the innate genetic tendencies to seek a paternal investment in men, women have a powerful emotional investment in a long-term relationship. Thelma knew intuitively how psychologists explain women's intense interest in marriage from a developmental perspective. The individuation process in girls requires severing a strong bond with their mothers, with whom they first attach and identify. It is a double task of identification and separation that boys don't have to go through. For boys, their mothers remain attachment figures, with or without separation. Their identification with their fathers does not interfere severely with the individuation process. In younger years, boys can date girls without attachment, have sex, and run back home to their mothers without ambivalence. Girls, by contrast, use relationships with boys as instruments for separation from their mothers. They need a new permanent attachment to give up the earlier one to the mother. Boys never have to give up that earlier one; their becoming men and their relationships with their mothers are not mutually exclusive. Occasionally, though, what remains of the original attachment creates problems for their wives.

Thelma would not have been so desperate for men if she had cultivated friendships. In fact, such friendships would have made her more likely to find a man. Unfortunately, society's relentless insistence on romantic relationships generates a variety of "pseudolove" connections, at the expense of friendships.

Some people say they have lots of friends, but if you ask them to define those relationships, you'll find that they will not share their intimate thoughts, concerns, and emotions with these friends; they would not even yearn to be with them. They will neither rejoice with their fortune nor be hurt by their pain. King David, after hearing of the death of his dear friend Jonathan, sang a dirge: "I am heartbroken over you, my brother Jonathan!" If you are not at least heart bruised by the loss of a friend, then you were not a friend: your relationship had not grown past the stage of acquaintance.

Friendship is our alternate psychological home. Friendship is not an optional need; it is a requirement for personal development. Psychological intimacy is not given; it grows with time, commitment, and being together through life events. A casual relationship can grow into as powerful an intimacy as that seen between passionate lovers.

One can be friends with a number of people, but no two relationships are alike, nor are they interchangeable. The inclusion of a third person (even another friend) in the dyadic friendship will change the character of that relationship, and not by dilution alone. Even talking about a friend to another friend interferes with that intimacy.

Contrary to common belief, friends do not need to see each other regularly, or talk on the phone frequently, or write long letters or e-mails to maintain their relationship. Once established, the friendship becomes part of oneself, an internalized attachment. It can be active or remain dormant. After months, even years of no contact, two real friends can pick up their relationship exactly where it has left off, engage each other as if they were never apart.

Friendship spans a wide spectrum—it is not an all-or-nothing phenomenon. One can cultivate acquaintances and deepen relationships all the way to a "holy alliance." Such a friendship has its own unspoken, inviolate rules: it is reciprocal and open-ended; no exchange puts an end to it; there are no intended secondary gains. The target of one's gifts is the primary gain: love and affection. These gifts can be letters, telephone calls, or recognition of important moments with the other. If the gifts are given to promote something more than the relationship, the debts become burdensome.

Friendship is potentially the longest lasting of all relationships among strangers. Passionate relationships are often time-limited. Teacher-student relationships, by definition, are successful, even if they end more quickly than expected. Most every teacher becomes a bore eventually, especially if he or she does not recognize that attainable knowledge is a grand equalizer. Business-related friendships typically end with the end of business. There is an old saying about the friendship of partners owning a cow: The cow dies and the relationship ends.

In *A Return to Love,* Marianne Williamson describes the difference between an unholy and a holy alliance:

> *For an unholy relationship . . . each one thinks the other has what he has not. They come together, each to rob the other. They stay until they think that there is nothing left to steal, and then move on. A holy relationship starts from a different premise. Each one has looked within and has seen no lack. He would extend himself by joining with another whole person as himself.*

COLLAGE OF SELF: SURVIVAL OF THE UNFITTEST

Although Thelma's family moved around during her early years, they always lived in small, homogenous towns in the Midwest, almost identical to each other. In spite of the fact that they remained relatively uninvolved, they benefitted from these communities, which provided stability and continuity even to an unstable and dysfunctional family like theirs. Thelma did not fully appreciate that benefit, however, and decided to move to New York, expecting to fit better into the city's disjointed modes of life. But it requires much greater effort and determination to belong to a community, where heterogeneity is the norm.

Not only those with a family background similar to that of Thelma's but even those who come from stable families are relatively vulnerable without a mooring community. The crystallization of the sense of self requires not only affirming, validating parents but also a synchronous community. Only a family that is congruent with a stable and homogenous environment can prevent alienation of its individuals and maintain cohesiveness of the family unit. The identity confusion that plagues youngsters in large cities is only partly caused by the fragmentation of families; even the children of intact families are subjected to disjunctive lifestyles in large, diverse communities. What seems to be a deviation from the norm, and thus not necessarily a desirable model for identification, in small communities becomes an alternative lifestyle in larger communities. These alternatives become desirable for counteridentification, that is to say, convenient avenues to *reject* one's parents' values.

In addressing dilemmas of identity in contemporary life, Kenneth Gergen writes about the importance of the cementing of community. Perhaps the most common form of decline may be characterized as the *collage community,* in which homogeneity in life patterns gives way to a multiplicity of disjunctive modes of living. Collage communities are hardly new additions to the landscape; they emerge wherever people migrate. Their growth, however, is hastened by all the modes of social saturation.

Large cities, like New York, where the drift tends to occur, may benefit in some ways from this heterogeneity, but individuals like Thelma are likely to get confused. They easily lose the relatively affirming, validating quality of a small environment and end up reflecting the amorphous culture they live in. For them, balance needs to be provided by even closer ties, and by greater structure. The extended family, religion, school, and communal activities become even more crucial to offset the disjunctive influences of such an environment.

SEEDS OF SORROW ARE SOWN IN EVERY LIFE: COMMUNION MAKES IT BEARABLE

Thelma, in her isolation, thought that she was the only woman in Manhattan who was neglected by her mother, not loved by her father, and had no real friends and no prospect for marriage. She wasn't even sure whether it was a husband or children she was after or whether it was something else. Her struggle with these issues was overshadowed by the feeling that she was singled out and alone in this ordeal. "Why?" she asked. "Why *me?*" Her psychological transparency of self-pity, alternating with self-accusations ("I must have somehow deserved this"), made her less attractive to others and compounded her vulnerability. Every minor negative event threw her into utter desperation. If her nail broke, it was time to end her miserable life. In her few and superficial relations, people presented their lives as near perfect. It is a social contract not to answer the question "How are you?" with a litany of medical and psychological problems.

In isolation, one's sorrow becomes unbearable, partly because one feels singled out for pain and wrongly presumes that others are just fine. For that particular moment, such an assumption may be correct, but across the life span no one is immune from the vicissitudes of living. In fact, living is defined not only by its pleasures but by its sorrows: They are the fundamental elements of being in the world. We all lose our loved ones, get sick and, ultimately and definitely, we all die.

The loss of one's hair is not the same as the loss of one's job, and that, in turn, is not comparable to the loss of a loved one. Yet for some, not being invited to a party can be as painful as having an illness. Of course, when they are sick, these same people begin to think how foolish it was to have felt so much pain about such trivial matters. Ironically, the brain doesn't differentiate among negative stimuli. Wrinkles in one's neck may be as disturbing as the loss of one's eyesight before the latter occurs. The massacre and mass burial of thousands of Albanians may not cause someone to lose as much sleep as his own impending prostate biopsy. It is always worse if it is happening to you.

There is a lighthearted story of a man who cites to his rabbi all the bad things that had happened to him: His wife left, he was fired from his job, his kids are in trouble, his health is failing. The rabbi says, "It could have been worse." The man puzzled asks, "How? Rabbi, after all this! How could it have been worse?" The rabbi nonchalantly replies, "It could have happened to me!"

In contrast to isolation, emotional engagement with one's fellow beings makes one a part of the community and allows one to experience commonality of sorrows and pleasures. The sense of belonging dilutes self-directed preoccupation and deintensifies self-pity. It also allows for experiencing others' sorrow. Although this commonality may sound like compounding the problem, in fact it helps to transcend one's own pain by providing an alternative meaning to suffering.

An old Chinese tale tells of a mother whose only son died. In her grief she went to a holy master and asked for a magical incantation or potion to bring her son back to life. The master advised her to go around and look for a home that has never known sorrow. But wherever she went, whether hovels or palaces, she found one story after another of sadness and misfortune. Ultimately, she became so involved in listening and ministering to other people's grief that her own sorrow was driven out of her life.

BELONGING BY COMPASSION

Thelma's family didn't belong to any religious, social, political, or civic organizations. They reluctantly attended PTA meetings, as nonparticipants. "We are not cattle" was their philosophy. Thelma's mother was Jewish, her father was Lutheran, and although they professed an all-accepting attitude, they were both nonbelievers, subtly undermining each other's faith. Thelma's brother adopted Christianity, her sister Judaism. Thelma fell between the two faiths. She declared herself an atheist without exactly knowing what that meant. She was taught that love was traded like any other commodity. She had no empathy for any cause or people and was indifferent to their plight. She wouldn't hurt anyone either. "I am neither saint nor sinner," she said. She thought people who served strangers in a soup kitchen were rich and guilty phonies. She was not involved in any communal activity. She was an "individual"—although she couldn't easily formulate what that was—who wanted nothing from others and not to be expected to give in return. Her symptoms were merely her memories.

Excessive assertion of a philosophy of self interferes with belonging, and excessive expression of relational philosophy forfeits individuality; we have to keep both in check. Deep down we all want to belong through our own individual and cultural ways. Hagao Kawai describes how two speakers' opening statements to an audience from different cultures—Eastern and Western—highlight their attempt for union: The Japanese, he says, speak with apologies, whereas Americans like to begin with a joke. But these two approaches aim at the same result: to belong. "When people in Japan gather in one place, they share a feeling of unity, regardless of whether they have known each other before or not. One should not stand alone, separated from others. Therefore, when one becomes a speaker, one has to apologize, asserting that one is in no way different from others. In the West, however, even though people come together in one place, each person is separate from the others, as an individual. Therefore, when one becomes a speaker, he or she likes to begin with a joke, enabling all the people there, by laughing together, to experience a feeling of oneness."

TRANSFORMING PASSION INTO COMPASSION

No seed ever sees the flower.

—Zen saying

I asked Thelma what, if anything, really turned her on. Was she passionate about anything? She thought long. Maybe justice, she said, and fairness. "I think I was unfairly treated as a child by my parents and later on by my siblings. There was no reason for them to so obviously favor one child over the other. I wasn't even a demanding child. I think unfairness is a very damaging behavior. If I were a lawyer, I might have worked for the defense of poor people who couldn't afford to hire one."

I thought that was a good place to start: to cultivate that personal ethic and transform it into a communal ethic. That transformation of passion to compassion is one of the everyday miracles about which we occasionally hear or read. An old cleric lived an utterly modest life, invested his meager income, accumulated millions of dollars, and then gave it to an educational institution; a full-time secretary, who also has a large family to look after, spends one evening a week in a hospice as a volunteer; a retired teacher works as if he isn't retired, helping youngsters in a poor community—of course, unpaid; a woman opens a boutique with donated outfits to dress unemployed minority women, to coach them in self-presentation for job interviews. I am sure you could come up with dozens of such daily miracles.

Looking only after one's self-interest is the contemporary expression of the ethic of Sodom, and it is equally soulless. In his book *Original Self,* Thomas Moore says, "In order to have soul, we need to be taken from, and that necessary emptying requires some collusion on our part in the theft, some distraction that interferes with our intentions, some neglect in our defenses." He advises that one needs not only to keep the door ajar but also not to be so excessively preoccupied with defending the area that theft is not possible.

In one thirteenth century Turkish tale, the old and sick Nasreddin Hoca was trying to plant an orange tree. A passerby watched and said in pity: "Dear Hoca, why on earth do you even bother to plant a tree whose fruit you'll never live long enough to eat?" Hoca replied, "That is true. But it is truer still that I have eaten plenty of fruit from the trees that others planted." Mutual exchange—giving and receiving—is a basic law of nature. We live by such reciprocation, inhaling and exhaling, ingesting and expelling, being helped and helping, learning and teaching. It occurs on every level of existence, and serves as communal glue. Of course, we can do so maximally in universal interchange, like that of Hoca, or minimally in specific individual reciprocation, like that of Thomas Hobbes in the following story. In *The Art of Happiness: A Handbook for Living,* the Dalai Lama gives an example of this controversial philosopher, whose dark view regarded the human species as violent, competitive, always in conflict, and concerned only with self-interest. Despite Hobbes's negation of fundamental good in human nature, he was once seen offering money to a beggar on the street. When questioned about this uncharacteristic generous act, he retorted, "I'm not doing this to help him. I'm just doing this to relieve my own distress at seeing the man's poverty."

Neither universal nor specific individual givings are totally altruistic acts; they are the source of our own well-being. Seeking and finding a way of serving others is a powerful source of happiness. Happiness is in the cultivation of one's garden, says Voltaire in Candide's voice. But the ultimate serenity comes from the cultivation of others' gardens.

ONE IS MADE OF MANY

Thelma signed up to volunteer at the Legal Aid Society as a clerk-typist on certain evenings and weekends, just "to humor" me. I think she was also intrigued about the idea of intentionally serving others without any obvious benefit for herself.

After the first weekend she was totally thrown off. "What misery out there! There was a homeless guy who was arrested for exposing himself. He said he was just peeing in the corner, with his back toward the other people. 'They don't let me go into any restaurants or office buildings for it,' he said; there was this runaway teenager from Minnesota beaten by her pimp for hiding the money from him, and she in return pushed him under a car; a young, handsome boy who accosted a decoy cop; three black prostitutes, who were cheerfully defending their rights to sell their bodies to anyone they wanted; a guy from the Dominican Republic who stabbed his girlfriend because she wanted to leave him; and more. I was there both days, ten hours each. By Sunday night I was wiped out, not from the work but from the stories, which were filled with pain and suffering. You know, I forgot to pick up any Entenmann's. I slept only a few hours both nights. Actually, I felt a little elated. Now I didn't want to tell you all this, because you may think that is it."

I didn't think so. In fact, the following week Thelma began to complain. "This is too much for me! First of all, there is no end to this. Every day more and more of the same or worse comes my way. I am preoccupied with these people during my own working hours. They are haunting me in my dreams. Last night I dreamt that I was walking down Eighth Avenue with these black prostitutes, and a little later I was arrested for impersonating a lawyer. This is beginning to hurt me. I think this compassion thing was not a bright idea!" Thelma was experiencing good suffering—suffering with others.

The historian Joseph Campbell says, "Compassion for me is just what the word says; it is 'suffering with.' It is an immediate participation in the suffering of another to such a degree that you forget yourself and your own safety and spontaneously do what is necessary." This definition reflects a sympathetic and empathic reaching out to others. Therefore, compassion is the strongest of all communal glues, adhered with the knowledge that our suffering (as well as our joy) is intimately linked to those same feelings in others; it brings us together. As one wise rabbi reflected, when it is very cold, there are two ways to warm yourself. One is by putting on a fur coat, the other is by lighting a fire. What is the difference? The difference is that the fur coat warms only the person wearing it, while the fire warms anyone who comes close.

"You see, Doc," Thelma exclaimed, "I am kind of an atheist. To me Genesis is the story of a family more dysfunctional than mine. Furthermore, it is written by men and for men to perpetuate their tyranny over women. And what is that idea that Christ died for our sins? They just caught him for rabble-rousing against the Jewish mafia of the times. I don't understand how, with a straight face, one can say that this Jesus' schizoid, confused life could be a psychological supermodel. They got him too young. If he'd lived another twenty years, either he would have been in a mental hospital with full-blown psychoses or he would have had his own ministry and later on been caught with a prostitute in a motel, or become the chief rabbi of Jerusalem. This idea that his being crucified should awaken my heart for compassion is ridiculous. Crucifixion was a routine punishment at that time, not specific to him. And rabbis, oh rabbis. If a rabbi kisses you, count your teeth, they say. Is spending all my free time with these derelicts, whores, and criminals, trying to help them to beat the justice system so that they can go and repeat their behavior out there, an act of compassion for the individual or an act of conspiracy against society? And what do I get in return? I know you say I shouldn't expect anything, but do I need nightmares?"

If one's actions are in the service of the self, they bring plain satisfactions, and make one competent at whatever work one does. But if they are in the service of others, they bring a deeper exaltation. Our civilization's egocentric, competitive notions of inspired actions make us miss their societal service. (*Inspiration* means simply "inbreathing of spirit," not "exaltation of the spirited.") Some cultures require their members to seek inspiration for the sake of society. Examples include Native American sweat lodges, peyote sessions, and dances, or Quaker meetings, whose members gather together to attend the appearance of the indwelling spirit. Integral to these rituals is the social philosophy that you can best serve yourself when you are in service of the others.

Actually, compassion is a reciprocative generosity, although it may seem to benefit only the immediate receiver. It may begin there, but it doesn't end there. Robert Fulghum tells the story of Menon. When he arrived in Delhi to seek a job in government, all his possessions, including his money and ID card, were stolen at the railroad station. He was totally bereft and would have to return home on foot, penniless. In desperation, however, he went to see an elderly Sikh for help. He explained his troubles and humbly asked for a loan of fifteen rupees to tide him over until he could get a job. Without any hesitation, the Sikh gave him the money. When Menon asked for his address so that he could repay the person to whom he was now indebted, the Sikh replied that Menon owed the debt not to him but to any stranger who came to Menon in need. The Sikh explained that help came from a stranger and was to be repaid to a stranger.

ONLY ONE FOR ALL MAKES ONE FOR ONE

We are genetically designed for selfish altruism. Our minds, at times, distort this genetic principle, and we begin not only to behave as "one for one" but also to expect "all for one" (in other words, me). Such tampering destroys the matrix of mutuality, the very ground of existence.

The selfish person loses as he gains. Winning, while depleting others, has a natural dead end. Plain selfishness destroys the ground, to the individual's own detriment. All organisms are innately directed to protect their environment for their own survival. Only humans seem to have forfeited that epigenetic principle. Epigenesis is a stepwise process by which genetic information, as modified by environmental influences, is translated into the essence and behavior of an organism. It starts with impregnation and continues throughout life. For example, the fetus is genetically designed to survive in the mother's womb at her expense but not at her peril, because her peril would cause its own death. The fetus strives to gain whatever extra nutrient delivery it can from the mother, while the mother tries equally hard to counter such attempts. When the fetus-mother balance of power is disrupted because of one or the other's self-serving efforts, deliberate or biological, the survival of either or both may be threatened.

Kicking and kissing begin in the womb. The growth of the fetus is a prototype of conflicts between an organism and its environment repeated throughout the lives of all living creatures. And the conflicts are resolved with compromises that reassure the survival of their participants. When it is generalized, this epigenetic principle asserts that whatever grows has a ground plan and, furthermore, that from this total ground plan all the parts arise, each having its own time of special ascendancy, until all the parts have emerged to form a functioning whole. In such an ascendancy, one has to be concerned equally about the well-being of the ground, that is, the base from which one emerges. Anyone who succeeds at the expense of his or her natural and social community betrays that divine balance. It is only by being for all that one can be for oneself.

This principle is exemplified by a story of the great Indian nationalist leader Mahatma Gandhi. It was known that once he settled in a village he would immediately begin to serve the needs of its people. When a friend inquired if his reasons for serving the poor were purely humanitarian, Gandhi answered, "Not at all. Rather," he said, "I am here to serve myself only, to find my own self-realization through the service of others."

True compassion toward our fellow human beings simultaneously serves ourselves—it is a mutual healing. Such generosity of spirit must be extended to all things, not just other human beings, to be considered ethical and merciful.

SOUL GIVING

Thelma was getting discouraged. Not only was she having nightmares but she was feeling angry at some people at the Legal Aid Society, for she felt not fully recognized. Even clients, after they were rescued from the claws of the law, would thank only the lawyers, not her. "I never envied men, I mean like penis envy. But I think I am developing some sort of pen envy," she said. The lawyers themselves seemed "oblivious" to her "need for some token of appreciation." They were, she said, "all taking me for granted." Even there, she found herself working later than anyone else and again leaving the office with the arrival of the cleaning crew. She did have a revelation that she might have stayed so late, at her own job as well as the one at the Legal Aid Society, in order to overlap with the cleaning people. They were very nice to her. She remembered a German housekeeper in her childhood who was very attentive to her. "Bertha! Oh, I miss her," she exclaimed. She had not thought about her for years. "Why was she so generous to me when I had nothing to offer her in return?" Thelma wondered.

The human soul is a small reflective sample of a larger nature, with all its mysteries. Therefore, one must approach it with the same awe and humility one might feel in observing the skies. While every attempt at simplification will betray the soul's simplicity, every attempt to resolve its conflicts would forfeit its growth. The soul thrives in complex peacefulness and contrariness to norms. Simple peacefulness is needed only as an interlude. The path to this complex peacefulness is through *soulful* generosity, soul giving, which means giving without any condition, and even in anonymity.

The act of giving may be related to two interconnected sources, according to the distinction Joel Kovel makes in his book *History and Spirit:* egoic giving and soul giving. Egoic giving is giving in order to get specific gains of prestige, praise, admiration, immortality; it is setting conditions for giving. In contrast, soulful giving is free from the burden of conditions and expectations. It is Bertha's form of giving.

Abraham Lincoln writes of an unexpected consequence of this soul giving. One day he encountered a peddler who had obviously fallen on hard times and asked Lincoln to buy an old barrel of goods, mostly worthless, for a dollar. Although Lincoln could easily have brushed off the failed merchant, he gave the peddler the money and stored the goods he received in return. Only later, when he cleaned out the barrel, did Lincoln find among the old cans and utensils a full set of law books. With these he began his studies to become a lawyer and pursue his future destiny as president.

GOD HAS NO HANDS, FEET, OR VOICE EXCEPT OURS

"I told you I am not a saint, not God's agent here on earth," declared Thelma. "It is your job to help these people. I doubt that even He could do it. Otherwise He would have. How did they become what they are to begin with? Where is your God to prevent all that? Somehow He cannot be found when needed. If I weren't an atheist to begin with, I would have become one after having seen all these human tragedies."

In his book *Who Needs God,* Rabbi Harold Kushner responds to why God is so hard to find by asking us to rethink the question. Perhaps we are disappointed because we are looking so hard in the wrong place, and perhaps we are taking the task too literally. Kushner alerts us to the view that Psalm 146, for example, which tells us that God secures justice for those who are wronged, gives bread to the hungry, and restores sight to the blind, is not really a description of how God spends His time. Rather, if we concentrate on the context of each sentence, we can recognize that securing justice is a divine act, a manifestation of spiritual presence in human activity, whether the acts of service are feeding the hungry, supporting the poor, or comforting the sick and the lonely. In short, "They are not things that God does; they are things that *we* do." Similarly the sixteenth-century Catholic mystic Teresa of Avila said, "God has no hands or feet or voice except ours and through these he works."

It follows that an atheist is not a person who says, "God has no meaning for me," but one who is really saying that the poor and the hungry, or working for justice, have no meaning for him. The atheist, then, is not the person who denies the existence of a Supreme Being but the one who does not honor the value of love, courage, honesty, and compassion.

SPIRITUAL SEEDS GERMINATE
IN THEIR OWN SOIL

Thelma, in spite of her bitter protestations, continued her volunteer work at the Legal Aid Society. She began dating a lawyer a few years younger than herself, a second-generation Chinese American. They met at the society and worked together on a number of cases. He thought she had a knack for law and should either go to law school or become a paralegal, that they should become partners and take on city prosecutors. The day they had their first success—an immigration case—they celebrated in his parents' restaurant downtown. The lawyer's parents were obviously very proud of their only son, kept praising and needling him with their limited English. "He is a good boy," "no wife, no good," "too old, no children, no good." "Go Temple always, Chen is very good boy." The night they slept together in her apartment, he just kissed her and touched her breasts. A little disappointed but also appreciative of his gentleness, Thelma wondered whether he was gay. But her worry about the "go Temple, good boy" business kept her up all night. "Temple!"

A few days later they attended the Buddhist temple together. She liked being there, except for those rituals. She hated them in the church and synagogue as well. "What are these obsessive-compulsive rituals? Don't human beings have enough of their own? Sick!" she declared. She knew a few things from Eastern religions, but she took yoga and meditation as kinds of exercise and anxiety-reducing techniques, not as spiritual grounding. Thelma and Chen had their first fight about that. "I am not going to the temple to believe all those silly myths and to follow all these compulsive rituals. If I were going to get into myths and ritual business, I would have taken up that of the Lutheran or Jewish religion, my boy. Om, Ah, Hum? No way, my mantra is 'off, fuck off,'" she hummed.

Thelma totally misunderstood the purpose of myths and rituals in life. They are part of religion but more than religion. Rituals are the celebrations of our myths, the stories that comprise the process of living; they are indispensable for our lives. Yet for some reason the words *myth* and *ritual* have negative connotations in vernacular use: *Myth* has come to mean unreal, and rituals are considered obsessions. In fact, myths are felt beliefs of generations within a culture, and rituals are concrete enactments of those myths. They may range from our worshiping deities in temples to reading books to our children at bedtime. They are found in the most sacred and the most ordinary. Their seeds germinate in every soil— they just have to be sown.

There is a major difference between obsessive compulsion and ritual. Obsessive compulsions are mechanical obedience to one's neurotic needs, involuntary coupling of thought and behavior to ease psychological tension, without succeeding. They are chains on the legs, not halos on the head. Neurotic compulsions may carry personal (albeit unconscious) meaning for the individual, but rituals address our collective unconscious and provide communal meaning, serve as the cohesive bonding of the fabric of society. The rituals in churches, temples, or mosques are all geared toward connecting us to our past traditions. As the noted twentieth-century British journalist and author G. K. Chesterton said, "Man was a ritualist before he could speak." The ritual acts of lighting candles, fasting, praying, and confession, baptism, and bar mitzvah, as well as reciting a mantra, all have historical connections, giving meaning to the present but relevant only within a given religion and culture.

Thelma's strong reaction to Buddhist rituals is very natural. The reverse would likely occur if Chen were introduced to Christian or Jewish rituals. One cannot adapt to rituals of a religion or a culture without believing in its tenets. One cannot import rituals from a culture divorced from its religious grounding. The man who is often thinking that it is better to be somewhere other than where he is excommunicates himself, warned Henry David Thoreau, as he dreamed of Walden Pond.

For Thelma, it might be easier to stay home in Lutheran or Jewish religion. However, if she cannot stay "home," she should come to Chen's tradition and make a total commitment to it. She must accept the new home with all its ingredients: rituals, prayers, prostrations but, most important, believe in its spiritual grounding. In the East, mantras are the ritualistic equivalents of Western prayers. "Om, ah, hum," the most well-known mantra in Sanskrit, are not just relaxing sounds; together they serve an overarching purpose of spiritual footing. *Om* stands for the body, and the essence of physical form; *ah* for the speech and essence of sound; and *hum* for the mind. In one's recital of these spiritual sounds, *Om* is intended to purify all the negative actions committed through one's body, *ah* through one's speech, and *hum* through one's mind. By reciting mantras, the chanter is purifying not only him- or herself but also the environment and all other beings within it.

In the West these mantras have no spiritual grounding. They are frequently used as a relaxation method, a self-hypnotic tool. As a means of vacating the mind, they can paradoxically be a compulsive companion to mind-altering drugs. The real ritual, however, isn't an intended act, it is *enacting*. One has to belong to an anchoring belief system that generates the rituals. What is important isn't doing a ritual, it is *being in* the ritual. Thomas Moore makes the crucial distinction between genuine ritual and playing at ritualism—the personal intentions and preferences of the one performing the ritual are secondary to the traditions and rituals that emerge from the original source.

That is why it is difficult to inoculate a ritual of one culture into another. To Westerners, mantras are devoid of their natural historical connection. An extraordinary devotion is required to overcome this obstacle. The reverse is, of course, equally true. Even within one's own community, the rituals wouldn't have a meaning if the child were raised, as Thelma was, without the needed acculturation. Some families deprive their children of religious, ethnic, and nationalistic connections. Under the strong belief of internationalism or agnostic or pluralistic paradigms, parents disconnect their children from their natural roots and their history. If they ever come back to religion and tradition, these children invariably lack the inner convictions that were severed or never formed. Their commitment may help the next generation, but they themselves will be playing at ritualism. Incidentally, the more zealously they try to succeed in their intention, the more likely will be their inner disconnection from the rituals, which will ultimately become mere obsessive-compulsive behaviors. What is needed is not to adopt any ritual quickly but rather to seek the spirituality that inheres within the religion and culture to which one belongs; then the ritual will naturally follow.

RELIGION AS AN ORDER OF COMMUNITY

Thelma not only came from a family who gave conflicting, if not negating, messages about religion but also was subjected to the doctrinal compliance of her therapist, who, more Freudian than Freud himself, considered religion at best a mass neurosis. She could cite all the worst acts that religions perpetrated but not a single good thing. Because she had never belonged, Thelma never understood the importance of belonging.

Religion shapes and animates our great steps from birth to death, as well as the little steps of everyday life. We then spontaneously fit our daily experience into that spiritual order. The word *religion* derives from the same Latin root as the word *ligament,* which means "to bind." Religion binds us to each other.

The contemporary culture, by putting less and less faith in tradition, thrusts us back upon our own resources. The individual is left bereft and can rely only on him- or herself. In his study of existential philosophy, William Barrett has described the plight of "irrational man":

> Thus with the modern period, man . . . has entered upon a secular phase of his history. He entered it with exuberance over the prospect of increased power he would have over the world around him, . . . found himself homeless. . . . Religion, before this phase set in, had been a structure that encompassed man's life, providing him with a system of images and symbols by which he could express his own aspirations toward psychic wholeness. With the loss of this containing framework man became not only a dispossessed but a fragmentary being.

For such a fragmented person, "I" experiences everything as external. As Robert Pirsig's *Zen and the Art of Motor Maintenance* describes, he is here but he's not here. He rejects the here, is unhappy with it, and wants to be farther up the trail. When he gets there, however, he will be just as unhappy because then *it* will be "here." What he's looking for, what he wants, is all around him, but he doesn't want that simply because it *is* all around him. Every step is an effort, both physically and spiritually, because he imagines his goal to be external and distant. For wholeness, the goal is internal and effort-less; it is being home with one's homegrown myths and ritu-als—not merely experiencing *I* in relation to it, but being *it*.

Faith is an experience of being gripped by meaning that becomes a paradigm for one's way of life. Religion provides such a ready-made paradigm, for it is difficult for an individ-ual to formulate a personal one. A shared worldview is much more likely to facilitate an identity of a Being, embodying the spiritual power belonging to the group. The individual, only thus transformed, is capable of differentiating himself from the group in order to redefine his self and his faith.

As communities restructured their authority through sec-ular systems, religious congregations performed the role of communal glue—a shared belief system serving to offer cohesiveness of relationships. In the wise words of Rabbi Harold Kushner, "One goes to a religious service, one recites the traditional prayers, not in order to find God (there are plenty of other places where He can be found), but to find a congregation, to find people with whom you can share that which means the most to you."

Kushner says that storyteller Harry Golden makes this point in one of his stories. When he was young, he asked his father, "If you don't believe in God, why do you go to syna-gogue so regularly?" His father answered, "Jews go to syna-gogue for all sorts of reasons. My friend Garfinkle, who is Orthodox, goes to talk to God. I go to talk to Garfinkle." So deep is the need to belong that it can perhaps never be ful-filled on earth. Ultimate longing and belonging means being one with God and the universe. The Tree of Kabbala por-trays its growth having roots in heaven. Therefore, only by growing down can one grow up.

NOT "I," BUT ONLY "WE," CAN BELIEVE IN GOD

Marriage, children, friends, tribes, organizations, and societies also serve our need to belong. Even religions serve (at least in part) to meet humans' need to belong. The sociologist Emile Durkheim spent many years in the South Sea islands studying the natives to find out what religion was like before it was formalized with prayer books and professional clergy. His conclusion, which appears in *The Elementary Forms of the Religious Life,* was that the primary purpose of religion at its most rudimentary level was not to connect individuals with God but to put them in touch with each other. Religion is especially uniting because of its promise of continuity with the past and the future. Eternal belonging is exactly what humans are craving. It doesn't even matter that much whether one goes to heaven or hell—as long as one goes with others.

Those who worship in liturgical churches, says Peter Berger in his book on faith, regularly join in reciting the Nicene Creed. This starts with the virtually rote affirmation, "I believe in one God." His concern, however, is that if one steps back and reflects on what is being uttered, at least three problems present themselves: "Who is the 'I' that is affirming faith? What does 'believe' mean in this context? and, Who is the 'one God' in whom belief is being affirmed?" Not many individuals can survive this line of inquiry alone.

Liturgical reformers have changed the "I" in the affirmations to "we," because for most mortals acts of faith can occur only within a communal context. Only God-like figures (for example, the patriarch Abraham, the apostle Paul) were said to be solitary believers. Such grounding from within is difficult to secure alone. This is no doubt why the reformed officiant doesn't stand before the altar, looking forward from the congregation; instead, he or she now stands behind the altar, looking at the congregation. This reversal of the traditional sacrificial position is a symbolic representation of the belief that the sacred being who is worshiped exists not outside the religious community but inside it. The self thus is securely embedded in the communal matrix, which provides thereby the continuity of being that extends from the human community to nature and on to the realms of God or other sacred entities. The Protestant interpretation of the Bible's *entos humōn* (referring to the Kingdom of God) as "among you" instead of "within you" is the recognition that in order to have the Divine Spirit within ourselves, most of us may need to belong.

THE WAY OF SPIRIT
IS BELIEVING

———◆———

BELIEVING IN THE SACRED

BELIEVING IN UNITY

BELIEVING IN TRANSFORMATION

Do not tell us what "it" is, but . . . confirm that it is.
—James Hillman

BELIEVING IN THE SACRED

A truly wise person kneels at the feet of all creatures.

—Mechtild of Magdeburg

GOD DESCENDS, MAN ASCENDS

Jim, a middle-aged, religious man, a successful professional, was agonizing over being between two states of mind. He had been married for ten years to his college girlfriend and had a great attachment and emotional commitment to her, but no passion. He had had a number of short sexual liaisons and tolerated the inner turmoil that came with them. These affairs were never a threat to his marriage. "Was it Updike who said, '*Dust* rhymes with *lust*'?" he asked rhetorically. He felt guilty that he didn't feel more guilty. He and his wife had three children. His love for his wife was a deep affection, although he was not "in love" with her.

He didn't even know the difference until he met Carol six months ago. She was "number eighteen" in a procession of women, a junior colleague at work, twenty years younger. His passion for her wasn't limited to lovemaking; he also loved being with her, cooking dinner together in her modest apartment, taking a walk, or silently holding hands. He enjoyed just looking at her, her face, her movements. Kissing her lips was like eating candy. When they made love, she was simply indulging her pleasure, having multiple orgasms, seemingly paying no attention to whether he was enjoying it or not. But he was. Her oblivion wasn't neglect. She was totally there by desiring and being desired—there were no calculations about what she should do to please him, or what erotic techniques she should use to excite him. She was free from all techniques; she was just herself, and he couldn't ask for anything better. Her being herself extended to her conversation and all other behaviors. Jim, as he had in his adolescent years, was experiencing game-free intimacy, the joy and pain of being truly alive.

Carol's spontaneity contrasted so sharply with his wife's organized, structured existence that Jim thought he was dealing with two different species. His wife, Mary, was extremely reliable and predictable. There were no surprises; she dampened their excitement but also reduced the tension in their relationship with each other and with everyone else. She anchored him in his insecure moments, shouldered him during his uncertain times. If Carol was his alter id, Mary was his alter ego. He could count on her as he might a competent associate, a solid partner. In the best of all selfish worlds, it seemed that he wanted and needed both women. Although he behaved selfishly, Jim was far from being a selfish man. He didn't really like the situation he was in, he always felt guilty, and no matter which woman he was with, his thoughts were with the other. He berated himself for being a sinful monster and praised the good nature of these two women, aware that he was exploiting them and constantly cheating one or the other. These insightful self-accusations were presented with further self-degradation: he wasn't really a thoughtful person and did not deserve even to try to understand the deeper meaning of his behavior. In fact, down deep, he said, he was a superficial person.

He was diagnosed by an alter-id therapist as having an "innocence complex" and was urged to enjoy both women. He was advised by ministers and friends to give up one or the other woman, and each time he tried he ended up no longer wanting to be with the one he stayed with, becoming completely miserable, and making that woman equally unhappy with his presence. While his sense of guilt in relation to both women was painful, his "descent to sinfulness" was unbearable. Though facing his kind and tolerant minister every Sunday morning was embarrassing, facing God in the darkness of sleepless nights was horrifying. "I failed my family, my church, my God," he cried out. He contemplated suicide, "a further descent" into his spiritual impoverishment. He was now on a well-beaten path: "How can I find my way back to myself again?"

The descent of the Holy Spirit is a profound image in various presentations of the Annunciation. God descended to earth to impregnate a mortal woman. The mystery in this "God-size fall" is illuminated by the angel Gabriel's announcement to the Virgin Mary of her conception of Christ. In our ordinary lives we may reach very high planes, succeed in our undertakings, and learn a great deal about ourselves and the world. We may even become typical heroes in our journey, or God-like, if our deeds are totally holy.

But we also fail. Some of our failures are circumstantial, and some are related to our limitations as persons. Failures associated with the circumstances of our lives are easier to accept than those attributable to our own shortcomings.

Experiencing failure as a disgrace, a well-deserved punishment, or as a final devaluation comes from not understanding the mysteries of life. Soaring successes may define
worldly accomplishment, but only a spiritual descent
impregnates the soul, validating not only one's human limitations but one's potentials.

The descent to sin can be a source for ultimate exaltation.
Joseph Campbell gives the example of Pope Gregory the
Great of the sixth century A.D. The Pope was born of noble
twins who, at the instigation of the devil, had committed
incest. When his penitent mother set him to sea in a little cas-
ket, he was found and fostered by fishermen and at the age of
six was sent to a cloister to be educated as a priest. Gregory,
however, desired the life of a knightly warrior. He conquered
the country of his parents, where he won the hand of the
queen—who proved to be his mother. After discovery of
their relationship, Gregory remained in penance seventeen
years, chained to a rock in the middle of the sea. Although
the keys to his chains were tossed into the waters, they were
eventually discovered in the belly of a fish. This unexpected
event was taken as a providential sign: Gregory was brought
to Rome, where, despite his history of double incest, he was
elected Pope.

For Jim, the pain of descent did not need to be relieved.
Any artificial attempt to resolve his conflict would bring
about only pseudoresolutions and most likely generate
depression, anger, and a sense of emptiness, as well as frequent undoing of his decision. The guilt, the remorse, the
fleeting zest all were to be experienced; they were the ingredients of soulmaking. The solution was in his soul's fermentation of these fully experienced conflicted feelings and not in
a forced cognitive decision. This attitude may be a deviation

from our usual norms, but at times deviation from norms is needed for the revelation of truth. In alchemy, this was referred to as the *opus contra naturam,* an effect contrary to nature.

Life is full of such mysteries and sublime paradoxes. Instead of seeing our failures as just failures, we may seek the spiritual potential within them. Perhaps the most profound symbol of this sublime paradox is that of the god crucified. The body with its five senses is left hanging on the cross of knowledge of life and death, pinned in five places (two hands, two feet, and head with a crown of thorns). At the same time, God has *voluntarily descended* and taken upon Himself this extraordinary agony. Thus, God assumes the life of man, and man releases the God within himself. The same door through which God descends, Man ascends. In our ordinary descents, we may be offered a pair of wings.

ENTITLEMENT IS UNMET SUFFERING

Grace strikes us when we are in great pain and restlessness.

—Paul Tillich

Jim's wings came from an unexpected, if still painful, source—illness. He had always been in good health. Besides ordinary colds and flu, and an unnecessary appendectomy at the age of twenty-one, he'd had no illnesses. He didn't even go for routine visits to his physician. To his friends and his wife, who would urge him to exercise and eat carefully, he would respond, "Well, we are all going to die sooner or later. What is the point of lengthening my life and ending up in a nursing home, being pushed around by some angry and resenting caretakers, being a burden to my children? I would rather die young. You know, there is a final reward when you die: you'll never die again."

Jim's life was primarily designed around his work, although for the last six months he had often been distracted. His wife, who was fully devoted to their three children, constantly tried to get him to spend more time with them, without much success. He loved his kids, but even when he was home, he was always on the phone with his business associates. One day after he made love to Carol, he noticed a few drops of blood in his urine, but he didn't pay attention to it. Although the bleeding stopped, a dull, steady ache in his lower back stayed. He tried to ignore it and took some over-the-counter painkillers, but to no avail. Finally, he went to see his doctor and was diagnosed as having prostate cancer. Jim's bravura ended that day. First, he couldn't believe that it could happen to him, then he panicked, and then he went to a number of doctors, all of whom not only confirmed the diagnosis but also agreed on the treatment—hormone treatment and radiation, because the tumor had metastasized to the lymph nodes and his vertebrae. He was told that he might become incontinent and impotent, at least temporarily, and that the prognosis depended on the extent of the metastasis. He kept going to different institutions looking for a better answer. He just couldn't believe all this, as if he were in a bad dream or watching a TV show about someone else's life. How could he be impotent? Potency was one of the reasons for his existence. He was very proud that he could have an erection at the drop of a "female hat," except his wife's. He was told he might have to carry a bag attached to his penis. He knew someone like that; he smelled of urine across the room.

If he accepted the treatment, Jim asked the doctors, "What is my fate?" He was told that with treatment his life expectancy would be five to seven years; without treatment it would be much less and with increasing discomfort and pain. He was between a rock and a hard place, perhaps for the first time in his life. He thought about suicide again, sinful or not. The idea itself got him more depressed and panicked. Now all he wanted was to live, no matter how. Not only Nietzsche's but many people's lives have been saved by the idea of suicide.

SYMPTOMS ARE THE SACRED SIGNALS

Under the black earth,
I saw hands that arranged roses.

—Yūnus Emre

"I thought you said the punishment is included in the sin, Doctor," complained Jim. He was anxious in anticipation of the cancer treatment and depressed by whatever result it might bring.

In psychotherapy the patient is expected to understand his conflicts and his deficits as they relate to his life, and to identify and uproot them. The symptoms the patient experiences are considered the manifestations of these conflicts and deficits. These symptoms are to be cured by working them through via the insights gained in the process of psychotherapy. There is no question that a large segment of psychological problems lend themselves to such exploration and resolution. There are other schools of psychotherapy that may emphasize, to various degrees, emotional or cognitive or behavioral changes, and by their differing techniques attempt to bring about "cures." The most common are sufferings of patients who present themselves with anxiety and/or depression, the anxiety as a fear of impending disaster, the depression as the result of a previous disaster, real or fantasized. There are, of course, many other symptoms, ranging from sexual dysfunctions to physiological disturbances, from phobias to obsessions, from low self-esteem to grandiosity. In one fashion or another, nonetheless, anxiety and/or depression come along with the other symptoms.

Listening to Prozac (or Valium) notwithstanding, most therapists try to figure out what causes these symptoms and provide a curative program based on their training and experience, as well as their concept of the patient as a psychophysiological entity. What get lost in the process, though, even if the symptoms are "fixed," are the *signals,* the messages that the symptoms are conveying. Frequently these messages contain seeds of spiritual troubles, extraordinary messages from the depths of one's psyche, that one may be on the wrong track, in the wrong profession, in the wrong relations, in the wrong town, even in the wrong house.

In our culture, symptoms tend to imply something bad. The word *symptom* itself, however, merely means a combination (*sym*) of accidental happenings that together form a signal of a larger happening, which is inherently related to the larger context. In this way, we can look at a symptom less anxiously, and more simply, as a *phenomenon* (a word that meant, originally, something that shows, shines, lights up, brightens, or appears to be seen). In James Hillman's words, "A symptom wants to be looked at, not only looked into." A restructuring of perception is what doctors are therefore urged to do, in a light that shifts the valences from curse to blessing.

Battle with an illness generates a certain strength previously unknown to the person afflicted and often changes him so drastically that his intimates are so surprised they may ask themselves, "Is this the same person I knew?" His self becomes transformed to such a degree that he could have a different identity, a different name. In fact, there is a belief among the Inuits that when you fall ill your usual name leaves you. Similarly, Jacob wrestled with the forces (the angel) that inflicted serious wounds on him. Although he limped from the scene, he had been given, in Homeric terms, an enabling wound and received a new name, "Israel, the God wrestler."

"You have no idea of the depths of my ignorance, Doctor, and there is no user's guide that comes with life." Jim pleaded. "Is there anything, psychologically I mean, that I should be doing or thinking? Please give me an unconscious hand." Jim was obviously referring to the conflict of being with two women. A healer may name the illness from its symptoms and make them visible to his patient, but the signals of the symptoms are delivered only to the recipient.

The lending hand of a healer could lighten the burden of the patient, especially if he is already a weight-carrying member of the spiritual community. But, ultimately, the person must first shift the valence of his life from suffering to calling.

In the tragedy *Macbeth,* Shakespeare writes,

> Macbeth: How does your patient?
> Doctor: Not so sick my Lord,
> As she is troubled with thick-coming fancies,
> That keep her from the rest.
> Macbeth: Cure her of that;
> Canst thou not minister to a mind diseased;
> Pluck from the memory a rooted sorrow;
> Raze out the written troubles of the brain;
> And with some oblivious antidote,

Cleanse the stuffed bosom of that perilous stuff
Which weighs upon the heart.

Doctor: Therein the patient must minister to himself.

Jim very much understood what he had to minister to himself as the hero of his own story. Although he and Carol kept meeting as if nothing had changed, everything had changed. "Can our relationship survive without sex?" he wondered. Weren't the wonderful cooking and all the walks together preludes to sex? Weren't their spontaneous behaviors manifestations of their sexual confidence? Carol kept insisting that the sex didn't matter; she loved him and she'd take care of him regardless. But somehow he wasn't comforted by her promises. He felt pitied. In contrast, Mary never made such a promise, although he knew it was implicit in their relationship.

One night, Carol prepared his favorite dish, steak tartare, and served a well-aged Cabernet Sauvignon. Jim bought two dozen red roses and a box of chocolates. Both exclaimed as they recognized simultaneously that this was the exact replica of their first dinner in her apartment. Instantly they understood that it was also their last. After the dinner, they lay on her bed fully clothed, hugged and kissed each other, and silently cried until the late hours. Jim drove home still crying. When he got there he tried to be as quiet as possible so as not to wake Mary. He gently eased himself into the bed next to her quiet tenderness.

GOD RETURNS TO US IN OUR ILLNESSES

Humans seem to learn the most fundamental things about life when we are about to lose it. That is, we are part of the whole, particles in the eternal existence. Our illnesses signal the need for realignment and give us an opportunity to reframe our lives. Illness, when forced upon us, gives us a heightened sense of sacredness about everything in life and the world.

Illnesses bring us closer to awareness of both our bodies and our minds. We do not fully appreciate the intricacy of the anatomical and physiological correlations in the body, its biochemical synergy, and its exquisite orchestration of neurotransmitters, *until* something goes wrong somewhere. A single cloud can obscure the sun. The disturbance in that delicate physical balance of health could be as minor as hyperacidity in the stomach, or as serious as a malignant tumor. The psychological effects range from difficulty falling asleep to disturbances of thinking or severe depression. We take our physical and psychological integrity for granted, because health is never felt. Curiously, most human beings are not that interested in their internal body parts, though they pay great attention to their external presentation. But when one part of the body begins to have trouble, an intensive preoccupation starts, to the point of exclusive attentiveness and search for healing of the diseased part. If the disease is a reversible one, it'll be forgotten as soon as normality returns and the person again becomes oblivious to that internal machinery, as if it doesn't belong to him or her. Even some physicians who are familiar with body functions don't take a few seconds to think of their lungs after pneumonia, or their hearts after recovery from an attack, and may continue their old eating habits, neglect exercise, and even smoke.

The mind doesn't comprehend the healthy body and is indifferent to its normal functioning. Otherwise, we would be ever grateful that we can see the golden leaves of autumn, the blue skies of summer, the calm snowflakes in winter, and the bursting forsythias in the spring. We would deeply appreciate hearing the chirping of birds, the laughter of children, the whispers of our lovers, or Beethoven's overture to *King Stephen*. We would be amazed that we can walk, run, wash ourselves, open a box, write, prepare food, or simply get out of bed. Until we lose any one of these functions we are not conscious of them, except in rare circumstances when we are awed by some emotionally powerful moment, recognizing these greatest gifts of God. Instead of waiting for such infrequent times, if we could stop for a few minutes and contemplate what we possess, the extraordinary qualities of body and mind, we would walk away with great smiles on our faces and gratefulness in our hearts. This awesome generosity of nature and God could lift any spirit, if we allowed that awareness to come in. In illness, that awareness occurs spontaneously (albeit belatedly). In health, one must make an effort to keep it.

"I follow your advice of loving life and also holding it loosely," Jim says these days with serene indifference. "My adaptation to indignities of living is honeycombed with ambiguities," he tells me, stressing the word *honey*. This is what is called health in death. Yes, his back still hurts, but he realizes that his legs and arms don't. True, he cannot yet have an erection, but he can hug and kiss. True, he still smells a little, but his hands are capable of washing himself. His prostate and its related system were in trouble, but he appreciates that the rest of his body parts are in good shape. Every night before sleep he reviews not what is *wrong* with his body but what is *right;* not what is broken but what is not. He gives thanks for his divine discontent and is confident that whoever brought him here will take him home.

Thus armed he continues building his life. In the words of Rudyard Kipling:

> *Watch the things you gave your life to, broken,*
> *And stoop and build 'em up with worn-out tools.*

Everything that Jim lived for in the past no longer makes sense. He does not care about making more money or socializing for business purposes. He does not want to waste time with people he doesn't like. If he has at least five years to live, then he has to redesign his life. He has begun to spend more time with his wife and children and a few of his old friends. He goes to watch and cheer his children's every game. The most amazing aspect of this change of direction is that he really enjoys all these activities, which he had neglected (if not avoided) when he sought excitement and purpose elsewhere. He is occasionally saddened that he'll be leaving these wonderful people sooner than he expected. But every day he is alive, he is simply grateful.

IN PRAISE OF THE MELANCHOLY OF AGING

Christy, a forty-eight-year-old married woman with a seventeen-year-old son, initially consulted me because a girlfriend of hers had benefited from a consultation with me during her premenopausal years.

In the first interview, Christy spoke of her relationship with Trent, her surgeon husband. She reported that the previous night, "I felt devastated. Trent and I were kind of frolicking in bed. He sarcastically commented on the increasing white strands of my pubic hair." Irritated by her hurt reaction, he launched into a long dissertation on the importance of telling the truth, adding insult to injury. "A truth that is told with bad intent, beats all the lies you can invent," says William Blake.

Christy, though a natural blond, had been dyeing her hair since her late twenties, so increasing white strands of hair on her head weren't as alarming. But was she supposed to dye her pubic hair, too? First, she got upset, then angry at Trent's cruelty and the unfairness of his implicit demand that she remain young. "He doesn't even have much hair left on his head, never mind gray hairs," She told me.

That night her husband couldn't maintain his erection, in spite of all her efforts, and didn't even notice her aching tenderness. "Am I no longer exciting? What is to become of me?" she wondered. "I don't have any career, and whatever few natural talents I had, schools educated them away. I got my Ph.T. (Putting Husband Through), was brainwashed to join WAM (Wife and Mother), and stupidly didn't pursue my operating nurse career." In fearing that she needed too much, she settled for too little. Even if she had a viable career, she didn't want that to be an alternative to being a woman. "I was about to say 'sex-object,'" she said laughingly.

She continued, "I am not alone on that. I have friends who are doctors, lawyers, economists; they all would rather be beautiful than professional, if they had a choice. Beauty is the only coherent philosophy woman has, believe me. They say if teenagers do not notice you, you are old. The other day we had an office party, celebrating the merging of two agencies. There were mostly young people in their twenties and thirties. As if I were invisible, people were passing in front of me, behind me, occasionally gently touching me to move me out of their way to get to someone else. None of these young people made any eye contact with me. I knew at least one-third of the people there. Even they just uttered a few words like 'Hi, Christy, are you having a good time?' and moved on without waiting to hear my reply. 'No, damn it, I am not!' I felt like responding.

"Finally, an older, inebriated guy from the other agency approached me and asked whether I was on the bride's or groom's side. Seeing the puzzled look on my face, he gleefully explained, with the help of his obscenely interlocking fingers, I was either on the screwer or the screwed side. As incredible as it may sound, I was rather content being with him, in spite of this inane conversation. At least someone was relating to me. But even this drunk, obnoxious guy was constantly screening the room over my shoulder, I guess to find a younger one to accost. He must have, as he eased himself away, interrupting himself midsentence—'We must circulate'—and lunged toward a buxom young thing. I saw Phyllis, an even older colleague, feeding her face with hors d'oeuvres. I tapped her on the shoulder and asked whether it was my breath. She immediately understood what I was talking about. 'No,' she said knowingly, 'it is your birth date.' I hate getting old. These wrinkles were to indicate where the smiles have been? Ha! This therapist I went to urged that I face the inevitability of growing maturity. I hate maturity."

Christy's reaction to her getting older was, in some ways, worse than the fact of getting older itself. Instead of experiencing dignified melancholy resonating with her aging, she was angrily fighting it. Instead of seeking the joys in the sacredness of her maturity, she was slipping into a kind of neurosis of aging.

In ancient Greece, depression was identified with the god Saturn. If a young person got depressed, he was called a child of Saturn, and he was believed to have suffered an aging of his soul. Otherwise, every adult eventually would reach a natural Saturn—the melancholy of the loss of youth. The vitality and sensuality of everyday life with its colorful existence would fade away, and the older person would carry a dignified halo of sacred melancholy around him, not unlike the rings of the planet Saturn.

Those who do not come to terms with their age may get away with it for a few years. Eventually, however, disappointments, rejection, and even ridicule will mercilessly tear down the fantasy of eternal youth, making holes in one's assumptions and illusions, and generating fears bordering on panic and fragmentation.

My father once told me an amusing but painful story about Jean-Paul Sartre's encounter with his own aging. Sartre was known as a flirt and a womanizer. Throughout his youth he lived as a ladies' man. His activities, including his numerous writings, all were subordinated to his interest in women. He would accept or refuse speaking arrangements not on the basis of whether the audience would be intellectually challenging, or whether the fee was high enough, but on the basis of whether it would be largely a female audience, and more so, whether the talk was organized in such a way that he would be able to intermingle with them socially before or after the talk, and, hopefully, seduce one or two. Even though physically he was not an attractive man, most women responded to his seductions, and he had many affairs. He never stopped chasing women. Unless he was loved by the last woman he wanted, he felt unlovable. Thus, he was in a chronic state of pursuing women, always anxious in anticipation and depressed afterward, regardless of the outcome. As he was aging, his preoccupation with desirability intensified. One day in Paris, as he entered a crowded bus, he saw a young woman sitting in the front. He elbowed himself toward her. For a moment as he got the young woman's glance, he felt encouraged and struggled with other passengers on his way to her. Finally, when he was next to her, the young woman stood up and gave her seat to him.

If one doesn't age gracefully, one will age embarrassingly. Acceptance of aging brings with it a ripe sadness and a light anxiety, validating the losses that have already occurred. Denial of aging brings a raw depression and a dark anxiety, invalidating one's self. The feeling of melancholy with its slowly maturing influence will bring out the depth and flavor of one's character. One does not have a choice with aging, but one has the choice of either suffering from it or enjoying its benefits. These benefits are different from those of youthful years; nevertheless, they are there. The only alternative is the starvation that comes from inconsolable yearning for one's youthfulness.

The melancholy of aging gives weight and density to one's personality. It distills the various lifelong experiences into a meaningful whole, giving them a firm grounding. It allows one's thoughts, beliefs, and values to coalesce into a life philosophy. The frightening, immense emptiness that melancholy seems to carve out in one's soul is transitory, and it is a preparatory stage for the *sacredness of aging,* which will fill a much larger space.

SUFFERING IS EMBEDDED IN
ITS DIVINE WORTH

There is only one thing that I dread: Not to be
worthy of my suffering.

—Viktor E. Frankl

About four weeks ago Trent and Christy's only child, Michael, died in a car accident. He was just eighteen. Michael was one of four passengers in a car driven by a friend who lost control and sideswiped another car, jumped the road divider, and turned over in front of oncoming traffic. Miraculously, all survived with relatively minor injuries except Michael, who fell out of the car and was hit by many vehicles.

Christy, who had before worried about getting old, seemed to have aged ten years within the last month. This healthy, vivacious, spunky woman shrank and shriveled. She wished she had died. In fact, she tried to overdose herself with tranquilizers and antidepressants three times, and the last time, ironically in the hospital, she almost succeeded.

Trent took good care of her and arranged Michael's funeral but also continued to go to work after a short interval and even socialized. For Christy he wasn't depressed enough. "How could he smile, even laugh, when his son had just died?" she asked. "He says he has two different selves, one in private, one in public!" Actually, each person is entitled to only one self; otherwise he or she has none.

To put oneself in Christy's shoes was impossible. Even just being in her presence was unbearably painful. There is nothing one can say to Christy meant to be consoling or comforting that doesn't come across as banal. Unless you have lost a child yourself, even your empathy may sound platitudinal. Even if you have been able to convey the deep knowledge of such darkness and ease the pain a little, you cannot convert it to any peacefulness. That comes to the mourner only by her believing in the sacredness of suffering, a belief that the divine light is embedded in the darkest shadows, a belief that transfigures the pain to quiet serenity.

We do not know what is being healed with sufferings, says Gary Zukav in *The Seat of the Soul*. Each person who comes through this world is called upon, at some time or other, to bear some of the weight of the pain that befalls the world. To assist in carrying this pain a little farther for others is a precious calling, although it may also be experienced as a difficult or isolating time in one's life. In *Eternal Echoes* John O'Donohue tells of a subtle brightening that resides behind the darkness as he explains the meaning of the Cross in Christianity, an enduring symbol of the transfiguration of pain. Both pain and darkness were carried up the hill of Calvary so that they could face the new dawn of Resurrection and become transfigured. In this sense, the Cross and the Resurrection are united. One does not succeed the other in time or space. Rather, the Resurrection can be viewed as the inner light that remains hidden at the heart of darkness in the Cross. In Christian terms, there is no way to light or glory except by passage through the dark weight of the Cross.

Suffering is the shadow of divine light, and its embedded divinity inspires the ultimate harmony. One's progress from pain to harmony and darkness to light is found in the celebrated allegory of the cave in Plato's *Republic*. The myth starts with a somber portrayal of the human condition. Men sit in the darkness of a cave, their backs to the light, able to see only shadows on the wall they face. When one of the men turns around, he sees no objects but the light itself, the light that has cast their shadows.

PAIN IS INFLICTED ON THE WOUND

Some old traditions say that no man is adult until he has become opened to the soul and spirit world, and they say that such an opening is done by a wound in the right place, at the right time, in the right company. A wound allows the spirit or soul to enter.

—Robert Bly

The day Christy found a little lump on her left breast she wanted to dismiss it. She'd had a mammogram just six months before. In fact, the nurse told her that not only were her breasts healthy but they looked like those of a twenty-year-old girl. Yes, she knew that and kind of flaunted it. She would wear a dress a little too low cut and often lean over a little too far whenever the occasion permitted.

Christy was sure that this was nothing, a premenopausal cyst or something. Nevertheless, a growing doubt began to preoccupy her. Finally, she called her doctor, who made time to see her the same day. Yes, there was a small, hard mass, the doctor said, and ordered a new mammogram, which confirmed the existence of an abnormal tissue structure. A biopsy was scheduled for the following week.

Christy's anxiety began to overwhelm her. She couldn't sleep, eat, read, or even watch TV. She was convinced that she had cancer. She didn't enjoy being with anyone, including Trent, although she made a few phone calls to her friends and felt a little better in telling them about it. Yet each time she hung up, she got more agitated and made another call.

All the friends she talked to had stories to tell about someone they knew or had heard of who'd had either a scare or the real thing, and the ordeal she had gone through with doctors and hospitals.

The day of the biopsy Christy took three times more Valium than the previous days. It had almost no effect. Surprisingly, the biopsy was relatively easy, even though they went under her arm for lymph nodes. The results would be available in four days. They could just as well have put her to sleep for the next four days. Now she was popping tranquilizers and sleeping pills, and drinking alcohol almost continuously. Throughout her ordeal Trent continued to make his work a higher priority, with the rationale that he had to earn money for all these expenses. He bought her a diamond necklace with a matching bracelet that she had always wanted, but he wouldn't make time to call for the results of the biopsy and complained that she wasn't very appreciative of the gifts or very loving toward him. Diamonds are fine, but love can be exchanged only for love.

Christy called her doctor's office the first thing in the morning of the fourth day. The nurse conveyed the message from the doctor that she and her husband should come together to discuss the results. Christy felt as if all the blood had drained from her body. She tried to call Trent but couldn't remember his telephone number. Her withdrawal from him was becoming symptomatic. Sometimes developing symptoms is the only way of dealing with another person.

The twenty minutes in the waiting room was like infinity. "Yes, it is cancer," said the doctor, but the good news was that the lymph nodes were not involved. "We could just remove the mass and do nothing else; or we could take it out and radiate it, or we could remove the breast and radiate it." He was clearly advocating a mastectomy and radiation afterward. The doctor and Trent were so matter-of-factly going through the ritualized recitation that Christy couldn't even listen. "I wish I had a woman doctor," she was saying to herself. "How would these men discuss, I wonder, the removal of one of their testicles?"

The doctor didn't know Christy's background or about her recent tragedy. But even if he knew, I wonder whether he would have conducted the discussion any differently. They say every nation gets the government it deserves, and, I guess correlatively, its medicine. In order to have the most high-tech, least expensive, most widely available, and most efficacious system, we have brought impersonal care, a term that has to be an oxymoron. Doctors are becoming interchangeable employees of an eight-hour-shift "health industry" (another bizarre term), which makes money by treating illnesses or, worse, making sufferers into consumers.

Christy's doctor had no idea of her emotional reaction to the news. Unless the doctor experiences the patient's sufferings, he cannot be truly helpful. This is not to say that the doctor has to be infected with the patient's illness in order to understand him or her better—though that may be useful too—what is more important is for the doctor to see himself as an extension of the patient, and to understand health as an extension of illness. The importance of this connection is easier to recognize in the psychological arena. A psychotherapist, who in his own life has had some familiarity with anxiety or depression, has had his own love relationships, and has himself suffered some losses and traumas is more likely to appreciate the suffering of his patients.

Of course, no one should be expected to be so unlucky as to experience all the misfortunes of life in order to understand every type of suffering. That may not be fair or realistic, or even as valuable as the therapist's ability to empathize with his patient, independent of the nature and content of the suffering. The healer need not be a "wounded one," but he or she must be a vulnerable one. The divinity of healing resides in that vulnerability.

As Trent and the doctor were discussing the pros and cons of various treatments, Christy just wanted to die. She didn't want to hear how many years each treatment would secure for her and with which possible complications. She wondered why this was happening to *her*. Hadn't she suffered enough with her only son's death? She was staring at the doctor's diplomas on the wall. There were snakes on the insignias. "Some symbol of healing art," she muttered under her breath. "I want to go home," she said, interrupting their discussion.

Yes, the unlikely symbol of a snake in healing art has its origin in the divinity of healing. In ancient Greece the snake was one of the gods' animal presentations. The snake bites where the wound is—the god would inflict pain on the wound—and if the wounded's faith remains steady, the sacred suffering will heal him.

ENLIGHTENMENT IS SIMPLICITY:
THE WISDOM OF ORDINARINESS

Christy opted for just the removal of the mass (lumpectomy), and no radiation or chemotherapy. She thought if she could survive Michael's death, surely she could survive a threat to her own life. Having chosen the least recommended option, she was on her own. She didn't mind; in fact, she felt kind of empowered by her assertion. It was her body, and she was going to heal it. She signed up for a wellness program. There she was given a large number of vitamins, minerals, and some relatively unknown substances. She would meditate twice a day and take yoga classes. She also eliminated all animal products from her diet. What other extraordinary enlightenment would she need in order to facilitate her self-healing? She wondered.

Only what happens to you is your sacred teacher, I said, following the observation of Berrien Berends, whether you get old, lose a loved one, or become ill. The secret, Berends says, is to learn to sit at the feet of your life and be taught. That means being constantly alert to your experience and always being receptive to life's teachings. I did not have much to teach Christy. Even in ordinary living, never mind for such Job-like sufferings, no one is really an expert. A good teacher sometimes knows that he has nothing to say. The best teaching emanates from what happens to the teacher and how he lives. That is why in a famous Hasidic tale of how to teach—and learn—a disciple goes to see his Rebbe not to hear what he has to say but to watch closely how he ties his shoelaces. I had no shoelaces.

Christy understood the task at hand and was determined to sit at the feet of her own experiences and heal herself. Self-healing through enlightenment is not a highly complicated, mystical, or philosophical achievement. It is a return to the simplicity of life. Transcendence isn't a supernatural striving but a potentially natural occurrence. Yet, by our psychologizing, interpreting, and medicating attitude, we treat ourselves as objects. Even our ordinary physical acts are laced with many unnatural layers. We don't simply eat, we dine, we have power lunches, we balance our diet. We don't simply sleep, we want REM, we want to record our dreams and bring them for interpretation. We don't simply have sex, we want to make a statement with sex, a commitment or its avoidance, we send messages through sex, we want to exercise power, display superiority or rejection. No wonder we frequently have problems in eating, sleeping, and making love.

No therapy, no medication, and no meditation returns us to our natural existence unless we stop searching or imposing meanings on our bodily functions. All these visceral functions are regulated by the "old" part of the brain, the subcortical system. The intrusion of the human mind, the cortical system, into visceral activities generates turmoil, not enlightenment. *The Tibetan Book of Living and Dying* tells this Zen story:

> *The disciple asked his Master:*
> *"Master, how do you put enlightenment into action?"*
> *"By eating and by sleeping," answered the master.*
> *The disciple was perplexed. "But Master, everybody sleeps and everybody eats."*
> *To this the Master replied, "But not everybody eats when they eat, and not everybody sleeps when they sleep."*

This kind of spiritual simplicity isn't an extraordinary occurrence belonging only to Zen masters. In *The Tibetan Book of Living and Dying,* such enlightenment is described as "something not exotic, not fantastic, not for an elite, but for all of humanity . . . it is unexpectedly ordinary. Spiritual truth is not something elaborate and esoteric, it is in fact profound common sense. . . . It is not being some omnipotent spiritual superman, but becoming at last a true human being." In this sense, it is no wonder that Buddhist tradition calls the nature of mind "the wisdom of ordinariness." Yes, our true nature and the nature of all beings is not something unreal and out of reach. The irony is that it is our so-called ordinary and real world that is extraordinary and fantastic.

THE SPIRITUAL HEALING: SACRED OPTIMISM

To one a foot, to another a fetter; to one a poison, to another sweet and wholesome as sugar. Snake-venom is life to the snake, but death to man; the sea is a garden to sea-creatures, but to the creatures of earth a mortal wound.

—Jalālu'l-Dīn Rūmi

The human mind can heal itself and the body naturally, provided that the mind makes room for the spirit to coexist with it. The healer, therefore, would help the patient to heal himself by simply helping him commune with the spiritual nature. Paracelsus, the great sixteenth-century Swiss healer said, "The physician is only the servant of nature, not her master." Similarly, the healer's role is not to impose upon nature but to observe, to appreciate, to witness, and to commune with.

Although her son's death and her breast cancer pushed Christy to the edge of rage and despair, since her late forties she had always been irritable and on the verge of anger and depression. Maybe it was postmenopausal depression, she thought. Her therapist scolded her for having adopted New York's secular pessimism and cynicism.

Those who are impoverished in their spiritual world tend deep down to have a depressive disposition. They steadily spew out anger and disapproval, and chant criticism filled with pessimism and ingratitude. The psychologist Timothy Miller purposely rewords a famous song in order to express such negative sentiment:

I see hungry kids and hopeless men—And futile wars
  no one can win,
And I think to myself—What a terrible *world.*

This is contrasted with Bob Thiele's and George David Weiss's first cadenza of their original song, "What a Wonderful World," which portrays sacred optimism, evoking gratitude in everyday living:

I hear babies cry, I watch them grow.
They'll learn much more than I'll ever know.
And I think to myself—What a wonderful world.

It is the same world, but perceived with two very different views. Miller tells us how to deal with this contrast in his book *How to Want What You Have.* When you are chronically pessimistic, negativistic, and ungrateful, he recommends that you take another look at the world. If you purge yourself of resentment, envy, or disappointment, you will find something to be grateful about. Such gratitude can be as obvious as being thankful for being fed, feeling warm, and being loved or as subtle as appreciating the small delights of nature. Gratitude may not naturally come to us because we seem to take for granted what we have. In fact, we seem always to be wanting more than we have. Miller suggests a simple practice of picking an object in your immediate surroundings and seeing "if you find a way that it might evoke gratitude." Christy, with a mysterious smile, said, "I tried. I picked one of my least favorite things in the environment— mosquitoes. And it was not that difficult to evoke gratitude. Aren't they food for birds, whose singing and sight delight us?" She began to cry. "Don't worry, I am not depressed or anything. You helped me to hurt better. Now I feel more intensely. They say middle age is a period when emotions become symptoms. These are tears of joy brought by sudden disappointment."

Christy, who had been just a social churchgoer, really read the Bible for the first time. She was amazed to find that, to a large extent, religious stories were about the cure of human ills through faith. In *The Uncommon Touch,* Tom Harpur says, "A study of the gospel reveals it is ultimately entirely about healing." In *Timeless Healing,* Herbert Benson refers to the Holy Qur'an, which says, "And I heal the blind and the leprous, and bring the dead to life with Allah's permission and I inform you of what you should eat and what you should store in your houses; most surely there is a sign in this for you, if you are believers." Similarly, a priest who commented on the faith healings at Lourdes, the famous Roman Catholic shrine, once said that we are mistaken if we think miracles produce faith. Rather, he insisted, it is the opposite—faith produces miracles. I knew from her smile that Christy was getting ready for a miracle.

BELIEVING IN UNITY

BOUNDLESS COMMUNION: WE ARE ALL ONE

The universe [is] the divine womb.

—Matthew Fox

Here are two poems, one from an ancient Welsh text, the other from a Sufi poet, thousands of miles and decades away from each other, revealing that same mystery of being in communion with the world.

> *I am the wind that breathes upon the sea,*
> *I am the wave on the ocean,*
> *I am the murmur of leaves rustling,*
> *I am the rays of the sun,*
> *I am the beam of the moon and stars,*
> *I am the power of trees growing,*
> *I am the bud breaking into blossom,*
> *I am the movement of the salmon swimming,*
> *I am the courage of the wild boar fighting,*
> *I am the speed of the stag running,*
> *I am the strength of the ox pulling the plough,*

I am the size of the mighty oak,
And I am the thoughts of all people,
Who praise my beauty and grace.

—"The Black Book of Carmathan"

I am dust particles in sunlight.
I am the round sun.
I am morning mist, and the breathing of evening.
I am wind in the top of a grove,
And surf on the cliff.
Mast, rudder, helmsman, and keel,
I am also the coral reef they founder on.
I am a tree with a trained parrot in its branches.
Silence, thought, and voice.
The musical air coming through a flute, a spark of a stone,
     a flickering
in metal. Both candle, and the moth crazy around it.
Rose, and the nightingale lost in the fragrance.
I am all orders of being, the circling galaxy, and the falling
     away.
What is, and what isn't. You who know
Jalālu'l-Dīn, You the one
in all, say who
I am, Say I
am You.

—Jalālu'l-Dīn Rūmi

I opened the door between my office and the waiting
room; there Philip, a forty-nine-year-old businessman, my
last patient of that evening, was furiously perusing an offi-
cial-looking paper. He frequently brought his mail to open in
my waiting room and filled my wastebasket with whatever

he wanted to throw away. The letter was a notification of a hefty fine from New York City for not recycling his garbage properly.

He frequently would begin, with a negative exuberance, a litany against someone or something as soon as I would open the door and continue during the first half of the session. He would not allow any attempt on my part to comment. This time, of course, it was City Hall that was the target of his opening salvo. "What did these fucks accomplish so far with all the recycled material, anyway? Isn't it sitting somewhere in Staten Island piled up? Why go through this charade, put people into expense and inconvenience? Even if they recycled 100 percent, which will never happen, I still wouldn't give a shit. Those highfalutin ideas of self-appointed ninnies, that we've got to keep the world as we found it for the next generation, are bullshit. How did I find this world to begin with? Polluted, hostile, and corrupt. Who built all those factories and dumped the toxic material in the rivers and lakes? Who tested atomic bombs and buried the radioactive material in the land of innocent people? Those high-voltage electrical wires, sprayings with chemicals, building dams—whose generation's ideas were they? Who brought the slaves from Africa, immigrant workers from Mexico, and contaminated our gene pool plus brought AIDS and TB? Where do you think these diseases are coming from? Who is smuggling drugs, selling and taking them? Do you know that half of the population of minority adolescents are in jail? The other half have managed somehow not to get caught yet. I think the police aren't really making any effort to get that other half because there is no room in the prisons to put them. And their parents? They are living on my hard-earned tax money. What is it with the Catholics and Orthodox Jews, and the so-called democratic nation of India, anyway—polluting the world with their offspring? No wonder the atmosphere is getting warmer. It would get that way from breathing alone. Never mind the food shortage; soon there will be no air to breathe and we'll be inhaling each other's farts! Life is a sewer, Doc, what you get out of it is what you put in." Philip was suffering from his own inner pollution, causing moral mutations on his psychological DNA.

"Previous generations never gave a fucking thought to ours," he continued, with a sense of urgency and the worry that I might interrupt. "They lived for their times, fine; same for me, when I die, the world will end. There is no such thing as an afterlife or before life. The hell and the heaven are right here on earth. The hell is other people today, also the ones in City Hall, and heaven is what I've already got, 'fuck you money.' Now did you want to say something?"

With Philip I experienced the inadequacy of highly praised common sense. He perfected the art of drawing the ultimate logical conclusions from an original misunderstanding. He couldn't find any solace because he thought of himself as an entity totally separate from the rest of the world. He couldn't see that he is City Hall.

In the ancient image, a drop of water in the ocean is indistinguishable from any other drop. The ocean exists only *in convivium* (living together) with all the drops. With humans, conviviality requires some degree of sacrifice of one's self-centeredness and joining as part of the communal life. It means focusing not on one's own success but that of the community at large, striving to own things not individually but commonly. That means investing one's energy and resources in communal properties, such as parks, museums, forests, lakes, clean air and water supplies. It means appreciating simple life, honoring virtues, promoting a measure of asceticism in the larger sense of the word and, yes, even as simple an act as recycling. We do have extraordinary examples of such conviviality by a number of individuals who would not consider themselves more than ordinary: Robert F. Kennedy, Jr., and John Cronin, Susan Seacrest, and Veer Bhadra Misha's fights to protect the world's waterways from being polluted; Mary Barley's work to save the Everglades from human plunder; Christine Jean's attempts to establish an estuary to harbor wildlife; David Kopenawa Yanomami's effort in the Amazon.

Philip came to me about three months ago with a moderate level of depressive symptoms, needing a "brand-name therapist" after he'd fired his eighth "generic" therapist. "She is incompetent and not smart enough for me. Furthermore, she is always taking Gertrude's [his wife's] side and defending Alex [his boss]." It was hard not to empathize with the people in Philip's life.

SELF IS FOUND WITHIN THE CONVIVIUM

About ten years ago Philip's then-fiancée, Gertrude, demanded that he see a therapist. Similar urgings apparently came from his bosses. They felt that he was too irritable, at times elated and volatile, at times too depressed, but always contentious. Since he had a brilliant mind, they all wanted to keep him in spite of his personality. Philip was in an ongoing battle to define himself by being against the world. He perceived his "self" under siege; he believed he would be totally swallowed by outside forces unless he vigilantly asserted his boundaries: "This is me, and this is mine." For him, conviviality meant losing his self.

One does not lose one's self by conviviality—living together with other beings and things—in fact, one can only find one's self in it. In his famous essay "Self-Reliance," Ralph Waldo Emerson says: "For the sense of being which in calm hours rises, we know not how, in the soul, is not diverse from things, from space, from light, from time, from man, but one with them and proceeds obviously from the same source." The subjective sense of self is best experienced by being part of a greater choir, by blurring or blending of boundaries between human and animal, or between animals and vegetation, light and space. Natural scientists agree with the Aristotelian thesis of a great "chain of being" that connects all classes of living things (as well as nonliving things) along a gradual progression of differences.

From animals, to vegetation, to earth, and to air, all is continuous and homogeneous. This homogeneity is not just a matter of form but goes to the essence, just as water becomes homogeneous with earth in the plant. The world and everything in it are close or distant relatives. In Robert Sardello's recent book *Facing the World with Soul,* he says that our bodies reflect the body of the world. In this sense, the human body is a universal body. Our cells correspond to the particles of the environment. Molecules that make up a human body, a tree, and a river are very similar. As we eat fruits, vegetables, fish, chicken, and mammals, they become part of us. Our muscles, skin, hearts, and brains are developed and maintained by what we eat. Ultimate processing and DNA differentiations are variations of the same existence. We are part of nature, no different from a bird being part of nature. At the natural end of life, our disintegrated remains have the same chemical components. We start with two mobile cell donations, and we end with millions of immobile ones. Although our ultimate shape is predetermined by the genes contained in these two original cells, the substance that sustains our spectacular growth comes from the environment. "We are what we eat" is literally correct, plus the two original cells.

Even illnesses are part of the universe. In their new science of Darwinian medicine, Drs. Randolph M. Nesse and George C. Williams suggest that diseases do not result from random or malevolent forces but ultimately arise from past natural selection. Moreover, perhaps paradoxically, the same capacities that benefit humans can also make them vulnerable. The authors give the example of autoimmune disease and its remarkable ability to confer benefits as well as endanger the body. Aging and death also are not random but rather are compromises struck by natural selection to maximize the transmission of our genes. One may find a gentle satisfaction, even a bit of meaning, from attributing the significance of our individual existences to a larger reference point: nature. Joyful and graceful life derives from the recognition, appreciation, and celebration of this unity.

NO-THING: LINEAR TIME AND SPACE
ARE MAN-MADE CONCEPTS

Philip didn't care about the future because he didn't believe in the future. While agreeing to seek treatment, he married Gertrude on the condition that they would not have children. He had her sign a legal document that if she changed her mind the marriage would be annulled. Never mind seeing any connection between himself and the world, he couldn't imagine one with his own offspring. He did not have any reverence for things that he needed to live for, or concern about preserving them for someone else. As far as he was concerned, life was meaningless, and eternity, God, and others were all just nonsense. He even had contempt for common sense.

If Philip believed in anything, it was his own mind, which also was driving him crazy. He was obsessed with time and reality, and his mind's relationship to them. As "meaningless" as his life was, he never entertained the idea of ending it. In fact, he was always in a state of mild panic that the time was passing by, that he was going to die. He desperately wanted to hold on to time. He was frustrated that he couldn't grab the moment, because the instant he identified it, it belonged to the past. "I feel that I am always behind the moment. If it is not now, it is not real. The fact that there is no real now, there is no real present. By the time I am aware of something, because of the inherent lag time, it is necessarily the past, therefore unreal. Do you understand?" It is one of the best kept secrets of the psychotherapy profession that when all is said and done neurotics are really, really incomprehensible.

John Wheeler, an eminent physicist, wrote, "The past, the present, and the future are all unreal as independent entities, but real as a unity." This recognition should tame our preoccupation with "now," our agony of the past as well as anxiety about the future. Philip's attempt at denial of the importance of the past and the future was his way of defending against anxiety. In return this anxiety deprived him of living in the present. He couldn't get beyond his mind.

The German philosopher Ernst Bloch has this epitaph on his gravestone in Tübingen: *Denken heisst überschreiten,* "To think is to go beyond," which means recognizing and going beyond the frontiers of thinking. The mind can relate only to what it can sense and touch, smell what gives scent, hear what makes sound, and see what is visually present. It can abstract and extrapolate, intellectualize and speculate. All this exists within the mind-made concept of time and space. If we look for things that can be seen, that is what we will see. If we look for things that cannot be seen, beyond the concept of time and space, beyond the enclosure of the mind, then the revelation of unity will come to embrace us with serenity.

YOU ARE WHO YOU WERE

"I have been in therapy for the last ten years," said Philip, "on and off, and with different therapists who were masters in making nothing happen very slowly. They all seemed to have come to the United States of America through the post–World War II neurotic exchange program from Europe, and any two of them could tell each other all they know in fifty minutes. Incidentally, with Freud being totally debunked, shouldn't all these analysts be recalled for fixing by their Viennese factory? Anyhow, they all tried to connect me with my past, especially my early childhood. For a while I went along with the travesty of telling whatever comes to mind, hoping that maybe there is a pony in there. My childhood was kind of a warped one, and my psychic genes were no better. Okay, my mother was a Nazi bitch and my father was totally castrated. So what? I cannot remake them; you see, I cannot do anything about it. The past is past. Most people are just nostalgic about the past, which they never really had. I resent the time and the money I spend talking about the past. It is *now,* if that. Can we just move on?

"An equally strange thing is people's fascination with history. I hated history classes. Who gives a horseshit what

Washington, Napoleon, and Henry VIII said, did, or didn't! They justify paying teachers of such irrelevant subjects by that phony idea that those who do not know the past tend to repeat it. Is that so, or is it the other way around? Isn't it that the hate among Bosnians, Serbs, Albanians, and Croats is perpetuated by their knowledge of the past? Who sent the fifty thousand men to be killed in Vietnam? Not the ordinary, uneducated farmer. It was the politicians and generals who studied the past wars."

Philip would get word drunk with his own transgressive energy and render his life down to a mere prejudice and mental promiscuity. "Lincoln gave freedom to blacks. Fine. Does it matter who gave it and when it was given? They have it now, let's get on with it. We still perpetuate the resentment and anger, guilt, sense of entitlement by focusing on the story of slavery. They are all free now to fuck white women. Is that what bleeding hearts, left-wing liberalists were fighting for? Well they got it! What then were we supposed to learn from the history of slavery? Don't let the capitalistic socialists run the country? Right? Now who is running the country and what pestilence is waiting for the next generation? Same bastards. I personally consider myself not even American, whatever that means. Today I kind of live here. Its present hardly interests me, never mind its past."

Cracking Philip's unconscious code requires remembering the old adage that when a man lies down on the therapist's couch, a horse, a crocodile, if not the whole animal kingdom, lies down with him. Philip couldn't see the connection between his misery and his attempts at denial of his personal and communal past. He adopted an emerging worldview of relevancy that defines himself cross-sectionally, independent of the past and future, individually or collectively.

Some people fear not only that precious time will be wasted in looking back, as Philip does, but that even a quick glance is a diverting form of sentimentalism or, worse, that such backward looking may paralyze the person and leave him frozen in time. Philip even cited the common misinterpretation of the story of Lot's wife to give weight to his argument: When God destroyed the sinful cities of Sodom and Gomorrah, he permitted Lot and his wife to flee on the condition that they not look back. But Lot's wife did look back, and she was instantly turned into a pillar of salt. Philip dismissed the alternative explanation: Maybe it was the torrent of her tears, her grief over her loss of the past, that turned her to salt.

WHERE WERE WE BEFORE WE WERE— IN COMMON MEMORY?

Those who do not look back deprive themselves of continuity with their own past, which forms the present. Our early relationships live in our current ones, even though we may not be conscious of them. Our present moods, thoughts, and feelings have a real a priori basis. It is known that our personal unconscious is formed with our own specific circumstances in life and powerfully influences most of our behavior. There is another, less well known but equally if not more powerful unconscious we all have: the archetypal—the collective—unconscious. It is multigenerational, inherited, and tribal. Together the personal unconscious and the collective unconscious form an individual's specific unconscious.

The archetypal unconscious is inherited in two ways. The first is the genetic one, through the direct incorporation of cell memories of previous generations. The genetically imprinted material passes from our ancestors to us through lineage. The "genetic" transmission in the memories of the unconscious is not limited to the actual passing of genes. Even through the transplantation of cells, one can acquire such memories. In fact, some transplant patients have reported a remarkable experience after having received a donated organ, such as a heart, liver, or kidney. Without knowing anything about the organ donor, they begin to participate in his or her memories!

The second form of archetypal inheritance is the tribal one, perpetuated through our myths. Some expand to the whole of humankind. Such mythical transmission of unconscious knowledge, experience, and memories is a collective source of the human psyche. At times only this archetypal perspective can deal with questions that are insoluble at the individual level.

Therapists frequently are puzzled and frustrated by the lack of success in their work with some patients, who may diligently regress, discover repressed early personal experiences and work through the conflicts of some of their personal unconscious but still maintain the symptoms and behaviors that brought them to therapy. This is because they haven't dealt with their archetypal unconscious. The archetypal unconscious always preempts the personal unconscious.

MYTHS ARE SACRED STORIES
TO GROUND OUR SPIRITS

Philip thought that everyone was a liar. It was just a matter of degree and success of disguise. He distrusted trust. Everyone was presumed guilty until proven innocent. He insisted that "some people, especially women, can't actually differentiate fact from the words, no matter how distorted they may get. The whole world, and especially its myths, is all lies. There are no fairy tales, white knights, snow princesses, witches, or Mr. Chipses. I first figured out this con game when I saw my naked mother arranging the gifts under the chimney. She didn't know that I was up all night waiting to catch a glimpse of Santa. The following morning I behaved according to my assigned role in the scenario. I learned the art of pretending."

Philip, in his need to debunk everything mythical and mystical or simply human, disconnected his roots from his collective past. His sterilizing truthfulness brought him an isolating impoverishment as he lived without dreams, fantasies, or playfulness. We need our collective past to frame our individual pasts and presents. Myths are part of our collective past. Not knowing and not understanding our collective past hampers our individual development. Mythology has a deep psychological significance and remains, in all its diversity, testimony to the profoundest depths of human character, both civilized and primitive, contemporary and archaic. When we examine its constant patterns and analyze its variations throughout the world and time, we can reach an understanding of the deepest forces of our psyche that have shaped human destiny and the patterns of our personal lives, validating not only our belonging but also our sanity. Philip's "insanity" was fueled, if not caused, by the lack of his conviction of these deep forces.

Our myths are our mutual philosophy. Without them we are alone. Their sacred stories anchor our spirits. They connect our personal experiences to larger human experiences. They join the present with the long past and the promised future. In mythology, we are part of the grander continuum.

NATURE IS OUR COMMON MASTER
AND TEACHES US EVERYTHING
THAT IS WORTH KNOWING

Philip not only denied and negated history, and people in his life, past and present, but also disparaged all other living things and creatures. He seemed to be hiding from nature, living an indoor life, except for walking to and from his car. As far as he was concerned, birds were pests, squirrels were rats with better tails, deer meant disease, and bear hugs led to certain death. "Why would anyone walk in the woods to get eaten by mosquitoes and ants, or poisoned with ivies and oaks? Jesus tells us to consider the lilies of the field. Obviously, he wasn't allergic to their pollens. You see, things have to be useful in order to be considered—like cows give milk and chickens lay eggs. What are the pigeons for?" Philip's glaring negation of nature prompted me to ask him whether it was related to his lack of knowledge or lack of interest. He replied, "I don't know and I don't care."

Joseph Campbell tells the story of how a Zen master stood up before his students to deliver a sermon. Just as he was about to open his mouth, a bird sang. The Zen master proclaimed, "The sermon has been delivered." Nature is a natural teacher. All you need is to read its sacred scripture. Philip had neither harmony with nature nor any idea what he could learn from this master. What a great teacher nature is, if one can participate in it. But Philip was just an observer, and a contentious one at that.

In nature, the observer remains an outsider. Hidden from nature, he can neither locate himself nor be located. The participant, by contrast, situated within nature, finds himself and is found, even if he is hidden in it.

NATURE IS TRANSFORMATIVE

Throughout history people of different cultures and religions have gravitated to their respective sites of power and beauty, such as the river Ganges (India), the Western Wall (Jerusalem), the Temple at Delphi (Greece), and St. Peter's Basilica (Rome), in order to seek personal transformation. Yet nature itself is the ultimate transformer. As Wendell Berry says, "Whoever really has considered the lilies of the field or the birds of the air and pondered the improbability of their existence in this warm world within the cold and empty stellar distances will hardly balk at the turning of water into wine—which was, after all, a very small miracle. We forget the greater and still continuing miracle by which water (with soil and sunlight) is turned into grapes."

In nature we are confronted everywhere, even in a simple garden, with wonders—but we have to seek divinity within them. In their book *Spiritual Literacy,* Frederic and Mary Ann Brussat advise us to spend time in a flower garden. But we are to make sure that our visit is long enough to take in the various charms provided by the universe of blossoms, stems, and petals. Whatever way we choose to spend our time, we should be aware that we are gracious guests in someone else's home—nature's abode—so we must act accordingly.

We should be bathed by the rays and feel the way flowers must feel as the sun shines on them. We should gaze at the great beauty and variety of blooms, their diverse shapes and colors, and the way each is different yet part of the world of flowers. We should use all our senses, hearing the sounds of blossoms in the breeze, and smelling the fragrance of the flowers, separately and together, and experience the garden's vulnerability and its infinity. If you really touch one flower, you touch the whole world, say the Sufis.

As Scott Russell Sanders says in his book *Staying Put,* one's spiritual center is also a geographical one: one cannot live a grounded life without being grounded in a *place*. By belonging to a landscape, one feels a rightness, an at-homeness, a knitting of self and world. This sense of clarity and focus, of being fully present, is likened to what in Buddhism is called mindfulness, what Christian contemplatives refer to as recollection, and what Quakers call centering down.

Whether at Stonehenge or in a field of flowers, human beings need to find a place to commune with nature in order to be grounded, so that we can afford to launch a spiritual pilgrimage. It is only by becoming a part of the sacredness of nature that one may unearth his spiritual self. It is there waiting for the transformation.

THE COMMUNION WITH NATURE

If you wish to know the Divine, feel the wind on your face and the warm sun on your hand.

—Buddha

Most of Philip's litanies seemed designed to protect his insecure physical and psychological boundaries. He was relentlessly attempting to define and rigidify them and to prevent any intrusion from within or without, no matter how benign or even pleasurable that might be. He was constantly asserting his interest, his agenda, his separateness, needing "hisness" to hold himself together, as if the interaction with the environment would render him a fragile fluidity or, worse, dissolve him into nonexistence.

We are all vulnerable, partly because we are totally exposed. As John O'Donohue says, although this very exposure allows us to have positive experiences, such as smelling the roses, seeing the waves and stars, and reading the hieroglyphics of the human condition, it also makes us feel unsheltered. His cosmic view is that one is surrounded by infinite space without physical shelter. This is why from the very beginning human beings have sought security, initially in caves and subsequently in houses. The desire for such strong physical shelters is a reflection of the sense of the openness of space, that anything can approach or attack the temple of one's life from all sides. Whereas home ideally offers shelter from this threat, it too is vulnerable. No man-made walls are strong enough to keep destructive forces away. Thus, the human body itself becomes a fragile home.

Ironically, the more human beings try to shelter ourselves, the more vulnerable we become. Only by being inseparable from the world does one secure his or her boundaries. Such a secure harmony is dependent on being in union with one's environment.

SACRED SOLITUDE: ALONE AT LAST, ALONE AT LAST, THANK GOD ALMIGHTY, ALONE AT LAST

One of the underappreciated lessons of the Greek myth of Odysseus is its reference to the importance of being alone. In that story, when his ship was torn apart and the members of the crew thrown overboard, Odysseus clung to a mast and finally landed onshore. His first words were "Alone at last. Alone at last."

One of Philip's defensive maneuvers against intrusions

was, paradoxically, always seeking to be surrounded by other people. Not friends, because he didn't have any and insisted he didn't believe in friendship. On the surface, he seemed to be a very social person, but in fact he was counterphobically seeking others to defend himself against. Reassured by their presence, he pursued his determination to keep his boundaries. One would think that such a person would rather be alone. But, in fact, Philip was most vulnerable to his most frightening feelings in solitude. Therefore, he made sure that he was never alone, which is why he got married in spite of his lack of interest in sexual or personal intimacy.

The deprivation of solitude is the cause of many manifestations of psychological and physiological distress. Being with other people for long periods of time, no matter how loving, wonderful, and interesting they may be, interferes with one's biopsychological rhythm. People interfere with one's synchrony with nature as well as with one's authentic self. Like all of nature, human beings are biologically programmed. Our psyche's interference with the physical rhythms and cycles is detrimental to our bodies, only to be negatively resonated, in return. This vicious circle is a distinctly human phenomenon. No other living creature steps out of pace with nature and survives. Chronobiology (the biology of time) asserts that our bodies have an internal rhythm or music, which we not only can but should tune in to.

In his book *Solitude: A Return to the Self,* Anthony Storr writes about the Antarctic explorer Admiral Richard Byrd, who searched for solitude in order to "sink roots into some replenishing philosophy." The explorer had reported that, upon being in the Antarctic at a remote weather base, he felt he was at one with the great natural forces of the cosmos, which he described as harmonious and soundless: "It was enough to catch that rhythm momentarily to be myself a part of it. In that instant I could feel no doubt of man's oneness with the universe." Similarly, Henry David Thoreau, in the quiet of Walden Pond, said, "When the whole body is one sense, and imbibes delight through every pore . . . I go and come with a strange liberty in nature, a part of herself." Both solitary men, in effect, found themselves in nature.

Solitude not only synchronizes the body with nature but also reinforces our belonging to a larger presence, setting the stage for enlightenment and transformation. Storr tells us that enlightenment came to Buddha while he was meditating beneath a tree on the banks of the Nairanjana River. Both St. Matthew and St. Luke report that Jesus spent forty days in the wilderness undergoing temptation by the devil before returning to proclaim his message of repentance and salvation. Similarly, each year during the month of Ramadan, Muhammad withdrew himself from the world to the cave of Hera. And St. Catherine of Siena spent three years in seclusion in her tiny room in the Via Benincasa undergoing a series of mystical experiences, which preceded her entrance to an active life of teaching and preaching.

Solitude puts the individual in touch with his or her deepest feelings and allows time for previously unrelated thoughts and feelings to interact, to regroup themselves into new formations and combinations, and thus to bring harmony to the mind.

In a reciprocal state, the more one is in contact with one's own inner world, the more he will establish connections with the external world. The more estranged or split from nature we are, the more nature seems dangerous and malignant, as Philip experienced it. People who tend to regard nature as a source of primary goodness and wisdom are more likely to experience instances of intimation of mystical union, and immortality.

In being alone, one can either be painfully lonely or in peaceful solitude. Just as one can be alone in the presence of someone else, one cannot be alone in the absence of someone else. One develops this solitude in early childhood in the mother's presence. In adulthood this ability to be alone is dependent on whether one has achieved an internal sense of presence of a reassuring mother. Nature can fill that maternal role regardless of whether one had such a mother. The capacity for solitude enables us, when alone, to be free to experience what is idiosyncratic in us.

The cynical saying that some people yearn for eternity but wouldn't know what to do with themselves on a sunny Sunday afternoon, never mind a rainy one, is not all that incorrect. We quickly jump to make phone contacts or arrange a date, to meet someone, at times even someone we may not enjoy being with. Being alone generates anxiety if one does not cultivate being with one's own self. It is interesting that people are often advised not to be alone, to go out, set up lunch and dinner dates, to avoid aloneness by every possible means. This advice is in part because aloneness is so commonly associated with loneliness. This misconception is what generates an anxious dependency.

In fact, if one can tolerate the first few times of being alone and not spend that time watching TV or arranging social engagements, anxiety eventually subsides and is replaced with an uncommon calmness—provided the person, in his solitude, reflects on his or her life.

The actual place and psychological activities this solitude would entail may vary. A great deal depends on the individual's skills and imagination. The context should be stable but free from content and form. Inner imaginations may take the form of writing, building furniture, photography, gardening, playing musical instruments, or the like. These activities emanate from within. They are the objectification of one's subjective state. They are not activities from outside, such as listening to music, reading a book, or watching sports. Those are also important, entertaining, and enriching experiences, but they are primarily taking in external life. At a deeper level, they embody the objective world. What generates a spiritual activity is finding an embodiment of the inner self and giving out to the world, in other words, changing from a passive experience to an active one. At times such activities emerge when one sets the silent stage for them by establishing a private space for solitude.

One frequently hears people complain about partners, parents, or even children who intrude into their "space" or do not allow them "to be." This need for psychological space, for time-out from relatedness, can occur as early as infancy. This *disengagement* is of equal importance with engagement at any age. If one lives in a family or environment that does not respect the need for private space, one can experience its absence as a suffocation of the self, a denial of personhood or, in Leonard Shengold's term, a form of "soul murder."

A private space is an extension of self and doesn't require an elaborate stone tower as Jung has described. All you have to do is identify a small area in the house, designed and decorated solely for your purpose and interest, wherein you can retreat undisturbed and uninterrupted. It could also be a specific outdoor place, in the park, in the woods, or by the river, a personally chosen temple where you can withdraw from daily activities and interactions in silence. Once you come to prefer the silence of a house of worship to all its holy activities you'll begin to experience some intimations of perfect harmony. As the writer and poet Franz Kafka said, in a similar vein: There, you listen. "You need not even listen, simply wait. You need not even wait, just learn to become quiet, and still, and solitary. The world will freely offer itself to you to be unmasked. It has no choice; it will writhe in ecstasy at your feet."

VARIOUS MEANINGS OF LIFE EMERGE FROM THE ASCENT OF SPIRIT

Just as the single light of the sun in heaven is a hundred in relation to the house-courts on which it shines; but when you remove the walls, all these scattered lights are one and the same. When the bodily houses have no foundation remaining, the Faithful remain one soul.

—Jalālu'l-Dīn Rūmi

All four months that he has been with me, Philip has alternated between anger and dysphoria. (Dysphoria is the opposite of euphoria, just below the medium.) He might have been a rapid-cycling low-level manic-depressive, although he never got clinically depressed or manic. During his dysphoric times, he would be hardly audible. He would talk about his aloneness in spite of his crowded social schedule, how he is sought after because of his money and, should he lose it, how no one would ever call, and even his wife would leave him. What was all this money for, anyway? He had everything he wanted, and then some. "Until now amassing money was my mission. What now? There is no one even to inherit my wealth. What is the purpose of my life?" he wondered. "The whole thing is meaningless." Then he'd start a litany against himself: "Look, let's face it. Everyone thinks that I am a genius. Actually I am not even that smart. I had no real education. I don't read. In fact I may have some sort of ADD. I am not even real. I fooled the world; I think I even fooled you. Can't you see I'm really a weakling, a scared rabbit, a worthless worm, a spineless leech? How did I make money? By marketing my psychopathology well: jewing people down and selling for more of some other people's sweat. Don't pity me! What is that look? I don't need your fucking sympathy, and don't you ever mention the idea of medication! Are you still here?" Was Philip a sheep in wolf's clothing, I wondered, counterfeiting himself?

There is no doubt that, without meaning, life is too heavy a burden to carry, even for the strongest among us. Kushner tells the legend that when Moses came down from Mount Sinai with the two stone tablets on which God had written the Ten Commandments, he had no trouble carrying them, even though they were very heavy and the path was very steep. The load seemed light because the slabs had been inscribed by God and were so precious to their carrier. However, as soon as Moses came upon the Israelites dancing around the golden calf, the story says, the words disappeared from the stones. They were just blank stones. Suddenly they became too heavy for Moses to hold. This legend tells an important life lesson: that we can bear any burden if we believe there is meaning to what we are doing.

It may be easy to empathize with Philip and even recognize some traits of his self-whipping soliloquy in ourselves, because the search for the meaning of life remains elusive for most of us. In listening to him, one gets a discouraged feeling that he could never find a purpose in life. It is as if he is condemned to this impasse of litany; that for him the search for the meaning of life seems simply an abstract intellectual exercise: he could neither descend by way of the soul to attain any practical union in life nor ascend by way of spirituality to attain any mystical union for eternity. Philip didn't even experience being alive, since he couldn't formulate some guiding idea of his existence. One's life philosophy is not an abstract matter; it has to serve one's daily life. Joseph Campbell, whose guiding idea was expressed as "the commonality of themes in world myths," was once asked by the interviewer Bill Moyers, "You're talking about a search for the meaning of life?" "No, no, no," he replied. "For the *experience* of being alive."

THE MYSTICAL UNION

The greatest threat to Philip's sense of control over his dread of dissolution came from his thoughts regarding an ultimate concept of unity. Therefore, he saved his harshest criticism and sarcasm for God and the prophets: "How could you seriously believe in prophets who are peddling some rosy picture after our deaths. Lions would eat most anything, but they drew the line at prophets." The idea of finally dissolving into One was so frightening to Philip that he made it a special mission to negate that concept. Of course, if God did not exist, he didn't have to worry about such an unmediated relationship with One.

Philip is not alone. Although many religions proclaim that ultimately all is One, not many people can experience this. A few may find themselves at that mystical center during occasional exalted periods, but most of the time we live on the periphery. Philip, as an extreme case, couldn't even tolerate being on the periphery. Thus he could find neither solace nor salvation. The ultimate salvation is making a connection between the ephemeral state of existence and the permanent state whereby we are absorbed into One.

The glue for this unity with the world is a kind of love that extends and dedifferentiates one from others, from things, and ultimately from the universe. John R. Howe, in *The Road Within,* asks, "Is there a ladder between Heaven and Earth?" There is no "here"; there is no "I" to stand independently. One does not view the world; one is dissolved in it. Enlarging our boundaries by loving is a gradual but progressive growth of the self, incorporating within ourselves the world outside. In short, the more we extend ourselves, which means the more we embrace the universe, the less clear and less important are the distinctions between the self and the world. In fact, we may lose our boundaries and become totally identified with the world. The closest we can come to this feeling of ecstasy is when we fall in love. But, as M. Scott Peck tells in his book *The Road Less Traveled,* there is a major difference:

> *The feeling of ecstasy or bliss associated with mystical union, while perhaps more gentle than that associated with falling in love, is nonetheless much more stable and lasting. It is the difference between the peak experience, typified by falling in love, and what Abraham Maslow has referred to as the "plateau experience." The heights are not suddenly glimpsed and lost again; they are attained forever.*

It is interesting that the confirmation of such "mystical union" comes from an entirely unexpected source—quantum physics. In his book *The Holographic Universe,* Michael Talbot points out that, although at the level of our everyday lives things have specific locations, at the subquantum level, location ceases to exist. All points in space become equal to all other points in space. Thus, it becomes meaningless to speak of anything as being separate from anything else.

BELIEVING IN TRANSFORMATION

There is no immortal entity but an immortal continuity.

—Anonymous

THE DREAD OF "NO LONGER BEING"

Ed was dying. Just four months ago, the day after his seventy-first birthday, he woke up with an acute pain in his stomach, which everyone, including his doctor, attributed to the heavy drinking and fatty food he'd consumed at the dinner party the previous night. But the pain persisted, getting worse and worse, and by the following evening it was "unbearable." Ed wasn't someone who complained about every little ache and discomfort. He never took painkillers, even after root canal treatment. He would brag about his tough army days and describe himself and his buddies as the "kind of guys who would go to the hardware store for breakfast." So for him to say the pain was unbearable, it must have been really unbearable. Ed, in fact, had to be hospitalized and put on a morphine drip. After numerous tests, he was diagnosed with pancreatic cancer. He was also told that this was a fast-paced disease that mercifully would not torture him for too long.

First Ed was in a good spirit of denial. He told everyone who asked him how he was the same joke: "It is like the story of the man who fell through a skyscraper window. As the man plunged past the fifty-second floor, someone asked him how things were going. He replied, 'All right, so far.'" But Ed was going through all this unfamiliar territory. The more assertively he distanced himself from the whole thing—the cancer, the treatment, the hospital, the impending death—the more the doctors seemed determined to have him get it. His last and defiant refuge under such a barrage of "truth tellings" was his conviction that they were wrong. "Okay, I may be sick, but I will recover, I always do," he would declare with sparkling eyes. If 80 percent of the patients with this diagnosis die within six months, then he belonged to the other 20 percent. And that meant they, and thus he, would live even longer than average people without any disease. How come this wasn't obvious to anyone else? he wondered.

As the pain got worse, however, and he started losing weight and strength, Ed's semidelusional conviction began to crumble. He was discharged from the hospital for home care with the not-so-subtle message that there wasn't much the doctors could do. He was told that he should be "home with his loved ones and in familiar surroundings for the remaining time." When I saw him at his apartment the second day after his discharge, he was lying in bed with an IV running. He looked bewildered and terrified. He wasn't looking at me as he usually did while talking. His anxious eyes seemed focused inward. "So," he said, "do you know, Doctor, what is really going to happen?" "What is it like, Ed?" I asked. "I am so scared," he replied. "I don't even know why. It may be just the anxiety of not knowing—the uncertainty." Ed was the kind of person whose every part from beginning to end was accounted for and gathered in securely. Now even the end of the road had disappeared.

Ed came from a mixed marriage. His father was Jewish, his mother a Southern Baptist who, though she converted to Judaism when they got married and promised to raise the children in the Jewish religion, never really followed through. She gradually reasserted her Christianity, began to go to church on Sundays and Bible classes on Wednesdays, and eventually became a deacon in her church. She taught Ed and his younger brother to pray to little Jesus and celebrate Christmas while allowing them to be bar mitzvahed. Ed used to joke that "I am not biased for or against church or synagogue; I play golf on Saturdays as well as Sundays."

But when it came to dying, he had to be for one or the other, which he couldn't do. He wanted to ride on his Christianity, wherein death has been likened to an illness or a physical trial that one must undergo, yet with successful passage one reaches a better world. There will be a transition full of fear and anxiety, but death, in fact, doesn't exist. What matters is not the fear of death but the thereafter—hell or heaven.

Then a Saturday-equivalent mood would sink Ed into dismissing the idea of afterlife and soberly attempting to cultivate a sense of resignation: that our eventual demise is inevitable, that death is a natural event that occurs in the entire animal kingdom and we have no choice but to accept it. He would quote extensively from philosophers who have provided a great many ideas to ease the process. Ed especially liked and would cite the well-known reasoning of the early Greek philosopher Epicurus, who says that we need not fear death because in fact we'll never encounter it. By the time we encounter it, we'll be dead. The French philosopher and mathematician Descartes, whom Ed also quoted, sought solace in the certainty of death amid infinite uncertainty. Soon, however, despite the philosophy, Ed became panicky, and he would convert to "Sunday Christianity."

All these wisdoms have their own respective truths, embedded in specific historical and cultural contexts. They serve to penetrate the centers of our primal sources, that inner drive to seek eternity or come to terms with its absence. Some people would say, "Well, we all die one day" or "We are all dying anyway," "No one lives forever," and so on. These statements are made either when one isn't seriously ill or when one is still secretly hopeful that he will survive somehow. Either way, humans constantly struggle between temporality and eternity. Ed looked deep into my eyes. "Can you tell me what is the best way I can deal with dying?" I told him the story of a man who was lost in a huge forest and kept walking in circles. Eventually, he came upon another person, also thrashing his way through the forest. "Can you show me the way out?" he asked. "No, not yet," said the second man. "However I can show you which roads *not* to take." These include denials, avoidance, panic, and desperate attempts to prevent death.

The human mind always seeks solutions to problems and occasionally finds itself in a complete stalemate. Death is one of them, the ultimate one. Human beings can't imagine our own absence. The concept of nonexistence for an existent being is, at best, baffling, like endless space or other universes. Such puzzlement precedes enlightenment.

When confronted with a fatal illness and given a short time to live, few can maintain any kind of personal philosophy. This is partly because the threat of imminent death changes a vague, abstract concept to one's own "no longer being." When one is forced, as Ed was, to acknowledge that one's own life is imminently disappearing, it is truly terrifying. There is nothing in our ordinary previous experience that prepares us for this experience. In the face of death, one seems all alone. No one is immune from this. In *Eternal Echoes,* John O'Donohue writes of Christ's predeath emotions: "Evident in his inner torture and fear in Gethsemane, something awful happened in that garden. He sweated blood there. He was overcome with doubt. Everything was taken from him. Here the anguished scream of human desolation reached out for divine consolation. And from the severe silence of the heavens, no sheltering echo returned. This is what dying is: that bleak, empty place where no certainty can ever settle."

LOSING SELF BEFORE FINDING IT

Where we are found or lose ourselves forever.

—W. H. Auden

"It came so fast; I am not even at the height of my obituary yet," Ed protested. "I still think of myself as a young man, far from dying. Finally, I had some financial security and began to indulge in some sense of entitlement. Now I have been told that I only have a few months to live. How could that be? I feel I haven't really lived yet, not fully. I was never free of worries to live fully. I didn't even have a sense of *how* I should live, except for external stuff. I am losing myself just about the time that I thought I was finding it. I made all kinds of compromises for the sake of appearances. Shit!" Ed's fear wasn't that his life was going to end but that it may never have begun.

The more closely our "sense of self" is tied to external factors, the more confusing death becomes. We know who we are if our identity depends on a collection of things, from our biography to our possessions, from our partners and friends to the tangible IDs we carry with us, just in case. It is on their fragile and transient support that we give form to the ambiguity of ourselves. When death threatens to take all that away, it's hard to know who is dying. Then, death plunges us not only into the fear of the loss of everything external we hold familiar but also into the dread of the loss of the unfamiliar: our selves.

Without these familiar props to rely on, we are faced with ourselves alone, selves we do not know, and sometimes even strangers with whom we have been living all the time but never really opted to know. Thus, in *The Tibetan Book of Living and Dying,* Sogyal Rinpoche asks, "Isn't that why we have tried to fill every moment of time with noise and activity, however boring or trivial, to ensure that we are never left in silence with this stranger on our own?"

Maybe we wanted to meet that stranger but never spend enough time to do so. We had time for everyone else but not for ourselves. Therefore, when we face death, we are entering an unknown territory not only without the familiarity of friends, roles, and possessions but also without *ourselves.* Fear is about losing what one has; the dread is about losing what one never had.

COMING TO TERMS WITH ONE'S ENDING

Let's not have a sniffle—Let's have a bloody good cry.
And always remember the longer you live—The sooner
you'll bloody well die!

—An old Irish ballad

Ed was so preoccupied with dying that he stopped living. He couldn't give an aim to his death, except as an orgy of self-deprivation. He rebuffed his wife's sexual advances, which was totally out of character for him. He didn't want to be kissed or even hugged. Sex and death are frequently contrasted because of their representation of life at its exalted moments—the sex for its joy, the death for its dread. Therefore, the experience of the union in sex sharpened Ed's false optimism and sense of disunion, the same disunion that he dreaded coming with death. He would get enraged by any pep talk. A friend of his ventured into the metaphor of a butterfly counting not months but moments, which was interrupted by Ed screaming, "Enough already!"

He wasn't interested in going to plays or movies, or just going out with friends. He even lost his interest in American Indian objects, which he had passionately collected over the years. He couldn't allow himself even minor pleasures of life, as if such indulgence would precipitate the calamity of death. If he didn't live, he didn't have to die.

Freud said that we do not have a concept of death and dying until the age of eight. I think it is more likely that not until fifty do we begin to understand that this life is limited and we are running out of time. We may experience the death of parents, and even some friends, and begin to experience the failing of our own bodies—weakened vision and hearing, reduced physical rigor, and increased aches and pains, all of which forces us to wonder about ultimate loss. Sort of. What prevents us from fully experiencing the possibility of death is an indescribable dread of no longer being. This applies not only to people who are comfortable and healthy but also to those who are sick and miserable. By any objective criteria, those whose lives may be considered not worth living still dread dying.

The Tibetan Book of Living and Dying tells us that we

should die peacefully, without grasping, especially if the cause of death is the exhaustion of our natural life span; a human being is like a lamp that has run out of oil. But when the need to prolong life is no longer warranted, we still make every effort to avert death. We make concessions, promises, and bargains with God, confess our wrongdoings, and ask for forgiveness. We still die. We die without full understanding of death, without truly experiencing it. Therefore, we forfeit this most powerful event of our lives, because we don't want to face the inevitable. The process of dying also must be lived.

Elisabeth Kübler-Ross, famous for her pioneering work *On Death and Dying,* describes the five stages the dying person goes through: *denial* (This couldn't be happening to me), *anger* (at anyone, including God), *bargaining* (I'll devote myself to ——— if cured), *depression* (Nothing works; helplessness and hopelessness set in), *acceptance* (resignation and coming to terms with the ending). Most people die while still struggling in one of the first four stages. There is always some melancholy of everything finished but very few come to terms with their ending with melancholy alone. Furthermore, acceptance means different things to different people. For some, it is concretely just putting their business of life in order—drafting their wills, preparing the proper transition of responsibilities, taking care of unfinished matters, saying good-bye to old friends and places. For some, the impending prospect of the end of life is a good reason to "drink deep from the well of the here and now." Such persons vigorously engage life for the remainder of their time, distilling from it the best with hurried zeal. They read more, they socialize more, they love more, they do more. Every minute now counts, and no time is wasted. For others, impending death prompts making previously avoided crucial decisions, undoing wrongdoings, expressing regrets, and requesting forgiveness. For yet others it means seeking God.

One can fully live one's life by recognizing its end, by focusing on death at the healthier times. In *From Beginning to End,* Robert Fulghum describes a caption for a photograph: "A man sitting on a folding chair in a cemetery, as a light rain fell and the sun shone at the same time, on the first day of summer in 1994." He muses:

> *He is sitting on his own grave. Not because his death is imminent—he's in pretty good shape, actually. And not because he was in a morbid state of mind—he was in a fine mood when the picture was taken. In fact, while sitting there on his own grave, he is reviewing his life confronting finitude—the limits of life. The fact of his own death lies before him and beneath him—raising the questions of the when and the where and the how of it. What shall he do with his life between now and then?*

We all need such full-dress rehearsals.

A SENSE OF NOT HAVING LIVED PREEMPTS THE EXPERIENCE OF DYING

Ed's dying followed neither the poetic condensation of Fulghum's man in the photograph nor Kübler-Ross's stages as neatly as she described them. Rather he fluctuated among the various manifestations of his attempt to cope with his impending death, without an orderly sequence or even any recognizable pattern. At times he was in total denial, at times in a rage or depression, at times he bargained, at times he seemed to be quietly coming to terms with the inevitable. He remained up all night to avoid anxiety dreams, while having "nightmares" when awake. Mostly he was in more than one of these moods and attitudes, and frequently in all of them.

At times he was cowardly, begging to live a little longer at any cost; at times he was bravely confronting death, either by total dismissal of its importance or by complacent desire for it. The braveness was identification with his childhood hero D'Artagnan (the young chevalier who befriended the Three Musketeers), who fearlessly fought many powerful enemies without regard for his own life and died in great dignity. Ed had always wanted to die the way D'Artagnan did. The hero would not be a hero if he saw death as terrifying; in fact, the first condition of hero stature is reconciliation with the grave.

Ed was very disappointed in himself because he couldn't face death as D'Artagnan did, but even more so because he had not lived like D'Artagnan. He wished he had shared more red wine and omelettes with his buddies, had fallen in love with the most beautiful waitress in the tavern, and had traveled penniless and sought noble adventures. He wished he were different. Ah, if he had had the chance to start anew! "I guess I couldn't have someone else to die instead," he said, not totally joking. He was known as being very good at delegating in business. With a self-mocking smile he said, "I can sink even further." One dies the way one has lived.

Human beings not only do not come to terms with whatever they are but never dare to live what they are not. Post facto they experience a sense of not having lived. They soon fall from womb to tomb, as does Stephen King's character in *Danse Macabre*. The real hero is the one who has lived his life as it was and fully—its everythingness—and when the time comes, which is simply having had enough of life, embraces death as a dissolution to nothingness. In the last chapter of *A*

Traveller in Romance, W. Somerset Maugham has his hero tell an interviewer how complacent he feels about the prospect of death, with ninety years of "hedonism" behind him:

> *There are moments when I have so palpitating an eagerness for death that I could fly to it as to the arms of a lover. It gives me the same passionate thrill as years ago was given me by life. I am drunk with the thought of it. It seems to me to offer me the final and absolute freedom. . . . I have had enough. There are indeed days when I feel that I have done everything too often, known too many people, read too many books, seen too many pictures, statues, churches and fine houses, and listened to too much music. I neither believe in immortality nor desire it. I should like to die quietly and painlessly, and I am content to be assured that with my last breath my soul, with its aspirations and its weaknesses, will dissolve into nothingness.*

Ed did not feel he had done enough of anything, never mind eagerly anticipating death, for he couldn't even go gently into his end.

DRINKING DEEP FROM THE WELL: LIVING WHILE DYING

> *And I who have been Virgin and Aphrodite,*
> *The mourning Isis and the queen of corn*
> *Wait for the last mummer, dread Persephone*
> *To dance my dust at last into the tomb.*
>
> —Kathleen Raine

If we do not allow the malignant fear of death to pervade our minds, we will instinctively extract every sweetness out of life, even at the moment of actual dying. Timothy Miller's book *How to Want What You Have* tells the story of a man who, in traveling across a field in the jungle, encountered a tiger. When he tried to flee, the tiger ran after him. When the frightened man came to a precipice, he caught hold of the root of a wild vine and swung himself down over the edge. As the tiger sniffed at him from above, the trembling man looked down to where, far below, a second tiger was waiting to attack him. He had only the vine to sustain him. Suddenly, he noticed a luscious strawberry growing on a branch near him. He grasped the vine with one hand and vigorously plucked the strawberry with the other. It tasted especially sweet.

To Ed, this story sounded totally absurd. "What difference would it make to taste the sweetness of a strawberry while you are about to plunge into your death? It is like asking a dead man walking what he would like to have as his last meal. I would ask for nothing! Well, maybe a wild mushroom omelette. What is a few more minutes, hours, or even days?" Because he couldn't live forever, Ed wasn't appreciating the moment. But eternity is made of moments. I dared to repeat the story told by Prince Myshkin, based on the Russian novelist Fyodor Dostoevski's own experience:

> *This man had once been led out with the others to the scaffold and a sentence of death was read over him. . . . Twenty minutes later a reprieve was read to them, and they were condemned to another punishment instead. Yet the interval between those two sentences, twenty minutes or at least a quarter of an hour, he passed in the fullest conviction that he would die in a few minutes. . . . He said that nothing was so dreadful at that time as the*

*continual thought, "What if I were not to die! What if I could go
back to life—what eternity! And it would all be mine! I would
turn every minute into an age; I would lose nothing, I would
count every minute as it passed, I would not waste one!"*

Ed apparently knew the story; he was listening with a grin
on his face. As soon as I finished he shouted, "But, my good
doctor, the story doesn't end with Myshkin wishing to live
forever. That fury of time actually got him to the point that
he longed to be shot very quickly. You see, I don't long to die
quickly or slowly. I want longevity, real physical longevity,
not your psychological longevity."

Ed missed the point of the story—the man wanted to die
in order to capture permanently that exaltation of the
moment before he was to die. The meaning of death is pre-
cisely its relation to the value of life. Ed was wasting his precious living time by his preoccupation with dying.

DEATH SEEDS LIFE: CULTIVATION
OF A PHILOSOPHY OF DYING

We all shall return.

—Koran

Ed was putting off writing his will in spite of his lawyer's and
the family accountant's advice, refusing to discuss the funeral
and burial-related matters, and not receiving friends and relatives. If he did occasionally see visitors, he would dismiss the
subject of illness and dying. The only topic he was interested
in talking about was the stupidity of his life. He cursed at
himself for having studied hard in school, worked long

hours, and wasted his time with charity dinners. Whenever people attempted to say, "But, Ed, look what you accomplished in your life. You have Beth, a devoted wife, and your daughter, who loves you. You built a business from scratch, created jobs for other people, you should be proud of yourself," he would get angry and accuse them of ignorance and insincerity. The family thought he was depressed. With their agreement, the family physician brought in a psychopharmacologist, who explained to Ed in a professional manner that "his feelings were totally in line with what is expected, that depression is a natural response of human beings to terminal disease. The depression depletes the serotonin system and is responsible for all your maladaptive behavior and feelings." The doctor prescribed some antidepressants, which Ed refused to take: "That lavatory, oh, I mean laboratory doctor, may be a great researcher, but I think I may have been his first dying patient. He needs to ask better questions before he offers remedies."

Calling in a psychopharmacologist to help Ed was like the anecdote cited by the French philosopher Jean-François Revel. "Imagine that a rock falls on your house, destroying it and killing part of your family. You call out the emergency services, doctors, and an ambulance, but instead they send along a geologist who says, 'Listen, what happened is perfectly normal. You know, the earth is always evolving, and there are always shifts in the landscape, tectonic plates crashing into each other. There's nothing wrong.'"

But if they had sent an enlightened doctor such as Louis Pasteur, he may have told Ed that all events are signs of the divinity, that his house will be raised again and his family will be dwelling in the house of God in eternity. Obviously, Ed would not have been so easily consoled. It is difficult to instill spiritual grounding at the time of dying if the person has not earlier in life cultivated the following tenets:

Eternal life is not mutually exclusive with dying.

Becoming "nothing" through death is the path to being everything.

Permanency is the result of a combination of transitory factors.

Primordial dissolution is the ultimate serenity.

One's salvation isn't waiting and hoping for a better life but rather an embodiment of all these seeming contradictions as a transformative unity. The writer Albert Camus eloquently said, "If there is a sin against life, it consists perhaps not so much in despairing of life as in hoping for another life and eluding the implacable grandeur of this life."

DEATH AS GRAND EQUALIZER

The race is not to the swift, nor the battle to the strong, neither yet bread to the wise, nor yet riches to men of understanding, nor yet favor to men of skill; but time and chance happeneth to them all.

—Ecclesiastes 9:11

Ed took his dying highly personally, as if he had been prematurely singled out. He asked, "Why me?" and "Why now? I can understand why Ashley [an au pair from England for his grandchildren] may be spared. But Harold is eighty-nine, Brooke ninety-something, even Beth [his wife] is two years older. They are all alive and well." Yes, but Harold, Brooke, and Beth will all eventually die. The tales of the loveliness of Ashley, the power of Harold, the nobleness of Brooke, and the loyalty of Beth will end in ashes.

Neither the accomplished nor the beautiful nor the strong, neither the rich nor the wise is spared from death. Napoleon died, so did Henry VIII and Suleiman the Magnificent and King Tutankhamen, not to mention Beethoven, Michelangelo, Shakespeare, Cervantes, Tolstoy, Picasso, Sartre, and Einstein. We may remember a couple of hundred people's names because of their surviving works or reputations, but there are other thousands, if not millions, who have fought gallantly for their causes, written beautiful letters, shaped and anticipated future scientists, artists, writers, and philosophers, whose names are completely effaced from our memories. If you aren't buried at Père-Lachaise, there is no guarantee that even your tombstone will survive for more than a few generations. For centuries the kings and queens were exalted, only to be erased from history. In his poem "Ozymandias," Shelley describes the remains of a statue standing in the desert. On the pedestal is inscribed: "My name is Ozymandias, King of Kings: Look on my works, ye Mighty, and despair!" Yet all that remains of the statue is the pedestal, two huge legs of stone, and a shattered body half-buried in the sand. Most telling, no one can remember who the man was. *Should* we feel despair? We might, were it not for the exaltation of the knowledge that death is the ultimate equalizer. Even the King of Kings is mortal.

Our complex bodies have remarkable built-in capacities for overall maintenance. Both blood cells and skin are replaced every few weeks, and some organs can be rapidly repaired if damaged. But we get only one permanent set of teeth in our lifetime. Although the majority of wounds heal quickly and broken bones can mend, some major organs—our hearts and brains—have limited ability to self-regenerate. And we are less well off than some other species in this regard. (Lizards, for example, can grow a new tail if the original one has been removed.) The bottom line, of course, is that our bodies are doomed to disease and destruction, usually within a century of their origin. So is everything else in the world, and most likely the world itself.

There seems to be a form of cooperation—or collusion—by the body with nature to limit its life span. All of our organs are in synchrony with that singular mission. All parts wear out at approximately the same rate, although on different schedules. Our bodies are not like the famous "one-horse shay" that fell apart all at once. Yet those who have actually measured the reserve capacity of heart, lungs, kidneys, neurons, and other diverse body systems at different ages have found that they tend to deteriorate at remarkably similar rates. By the time a human being reaches one hundred years old, virtually all systems are greatly compromised. Although senescence itself is not a disease, it is the product of every bodily capacity gradually declining and thus becoming more vulnerable to a panoply of illnesses. This means not only cancer and heart attacks but even accidents caused by failing vision, thinning bones, loss of coordination, and the like.

Regardless of how it happens, all human bodies—whether Ed's or a king's—are programmed to cease as functional units, and return silently to an inorganic state.

INFINITY IS A RESULT OF A SERIES OF FINITE TRANSITIONS

To see a World in a Grain of Sand
And a Heaven in a Wild Flower.
Hold Infinity in the palm of your hand
And Eternity in an hour.

—William Blake

There is continuity among King Ozymandias and the poet Shelley and us. Shelley read the inscription and resonated with the king's despair, bringing hope to us, the community of mortals. Similarly, Chopin's music resonates in our hearts, Cézanne's paintings reflect in our eyes, Rūmi's verses serenade our souls. These are just extraordinary examples of our immortality. Closer to home, you may carry the smile of your mother, or the melancholia of your grandfather.

All the particulars of precious, ordinary living creatures, famous or not, human or not, are still here, only transmuted into other forms. In this context of nature, death is only part of the larger cycle of birth and renewal. The seeds of today sprout, grow, blossom—and fall back, to be repeated in tomorrow's seeds. The cycles of endless renewal, however, are not beyond death—they embrace death as part of a larger plan or purpose. This is also true within our bodies. Our cells undergo aging and death, but not because they have been forced into extinction by some grim reaper. Rather, the atoms that constitute our being are billions of years old and have a comparable number of years of more life. When they are gradually broken down into smaller particles, these atoms do not die; instead, they get transformed into another configuration. From death comes life, and *only* from that death comes life.

No creature, writes Ananda Coomaraswamy in *The New Indian Antiquary,* can attain a higher grade of nature without itself ceasing to exist. Indeed, she says, "The physical body of the hero may be actually slain, dismembered, and scattered over the land or sea." He will return to nature to nurture new sprouts that partake of the cycles of endless renewal without knowing that would be his fate, something as natural as a seed or plant coming out of the ground. The seed has no idea of being some particular plant, but it has its own form and is in perfect harmony with the ground, with its surroundings. As it grows, it expresses its nature.

Our presence is impermanent and has been compared to drawings made on the surface of water with one's finger. Similarly, everything in the world and beyond is made up of infinitesimally tiny changes. This transitoriness is expressed colorfully by Jean-François Revel and Matthieu Ricard, as father and son discuss the meaning of life:

> *A rainbow is formed by the play of a shaft of sunlight falling on a cloud of raindrops. It appears, but it's intangible. As soon as one of the factors contributing to it is missing, the phenomenon disappears. So the "rainbow" has no inherent nature of its own, and you can't speak of the dissolution or annihilation of something that didn't exist in the first place. That "something" only owed its illusory appearance to a transitory coming together of elements which aren't intrinsically existing entities themselves, either. . . . Therefore all phenomena are the result of a combination of transitory factors.*

A similar insight is expressed in *The Tibetan Book of Living and Dying:*

> *A wave in the sea, seen in one way, seems to have a distinct iden-*
> *tity, an end and a beginning. Seen in another way, the wave itself*
> *doesn't really exist but is just the behavior of water, . . . something*
> *made temporarily possible by wind and water, and is dependent*
> *on a set of constantly changing circumstances . . . and every wave*
> *is related to every other wave. Nothing has any inherent existence*
> *of its own.*

Ed will not die if he comes to one of these revelations:
either he'll die only in his present form but will remain eternal in a different form or he will never die because he never
existed.

ETERNAL SELF RECYCLING

I take the earth as my witness.

—Matthieu Ricard

The total weight of all elements in the world remains stable.
The nature of the elements—for instance, the total level of
water and amount of calcium in the world—is also constant.
But these elements are capable of forming quite different
physiological beings, such as animals and flowers, and they
can remain inert, as ice or salt. Substances that make up living and nonliving things are one and the same. They are
interchangeably usable.

Although our physical body seems to be composed of solid
matter that can be broken down into molecules and atoms,
quantum physics reminds us that every atom is more than 99
percent empty space. Moreover, the subatomic particles moving at lightning speed through this "empty" space are really
bundles of vibrating energy. They carry coded information

for creation and destruction, temporally serving the needs of the host they inhabit but primarily serving transformative purposes, the perpetuation of the planet as an organism. When we look at the smaller picture within the larger one, we observe that in every cell some chemical reactions are anabolic; that is, they produce new proteins from amino acids; others are destructive, such as the process of digestion, which breaks down complex ingested foods into simpler compounds. Creation/life and destruction/death are in continuous cycle with each other. A living organism is being taken in by another, wherein new living particles are created or simply converted to energy for them.

Nietzsche presented a rational premise for the idea of the Eternal Return, that if time were infinite and the particles in the universe finite, then by laws of probability all combinations must repeat themselves eternally. Therefore everything, ourselves included, must recur again and again down to the last detail.

God's creatures are food for each other to perpetuate eternity. This is the sacramental mystery of food, although it rarely comes to our minds as such when we sit down to eat lunch. We may say grace before meals, but that's it. There were cultures where, when people would sit down to eat, they would thank the animal they were about to consume. This tradition is reminiscent of a joyous saying in one of the Upanishads: "I am the food of life, I am, I am; I eat the food of life, I eat, I eat."

While we are physically continuous in the great chain of food, we are also spiritually continuous in the great chain of being. There is the karmic theory that postulates a kinship between all observed species of beings, that individuals mutate through different life-forms from lifetime to lifetime.

Species evolve in relation to their environments, and even individuals mutate from species to species. This karmic evolution can be random, and beings can evolve into lower forms as well as higher ones.

We are travelers on a cosmic journey, says Deepak Chopra, "stardust, swirling and dancing in the eddies and whirlpools of infinity. Life is eternal." Yet, at the same time, "the expressions of life are ephemeral, momentary, transient." We are finite in the presently expressed form, but eternal in all potential forms.

THE WORLD IS ONE OF OUR SENSES

"What will happen to my project?" (Ed was developing a commercial site with Wayne, the architect husband of his only daughter.) "Wayne was always scheming; now he is going to take full control of it. He came yesterday to announce that he is going to name the complex after me. He already buried me, the son of a bitch! While he was presenting me with the final plans in detail, I couldn't even concentrate. I was thinking, What will happen to my ties? I have hundreds of them, some not even worn once! You know, it is the easiest gift to a man. So I have all these ugly ties in my closet. What about my passport, my watch, my private telephone book? Will someone dial each number and tell them I am dead? I guess Beth will have to erase my voice from the answering machine. Poor woman, what will happen to her? No one would marry a seventy-three-year-old, arthritic, diabetic woman. For her sake I wish she would die before me. She is totally dependent on me." ("Beth, Beth!" he yelled, "Could you bring that gray tie box from the closet? I want the doctor to pick one for himself. No, no, not these, they match my eyes. The other, yes, the gray one, that, that one, damn it!") "I think she is getting a little senile, Doctor, you may have noticed it, not that she was that bright to begin with. Our daughter has the same air head." Ed's life was full of interpersonal drama, which his sickness only intensified. "What is the point of all this?" he kept lamenting and offered to read a few lines from Ecclesiastes to validate his stand:

> *I accomplished some great things:*
> *But when I turned to look at all that I had accomplished*
> *and all the hard work I had put into it, I saw that it was all*
> *pointless.*
> *It was like trying to catch the wind.*
> *Then I turned my attention to experience wisdom . . .*
> *I saw that wisdom has an advantage over foolishness*
> *as light has an advantage over darkness. . . . But I have*
> *also come to realize that the same destiny that waits for*
> *the fool waits for me as well, then what is the advantage in*
> *being wise? So I thought that even this is pointless.*

"Even if it were pointful—is there just a word?" Ed continued. "Like Woody Allen I don't want to achieve immortality by my work, I want to achieve immortality by not dying." His sense of humor occasionally broke through his dark mood.

Of course, not just for Ed but for all of us, life seems to be an unending personal drama, and we are its permanent main character—until we are confronted with the inevitable: curtain time. Then we wonder about the point of it all. Not only our interpersonal dramas but all of our other daily struggles, conflicts, and worries are compulsions to support our illusions that we will be here forever. We lend our five senses to solidify that illusionary world of permanency. In fact, the connection of all of our senses to the world is the most ephemeral. In *The Tibetan Book of the Dead* it is said:

> *Nothing that we think we are, do, feel, or have has any essence, substance, stability, or solidity. All the somethings in and around us with which we preoccupy ourselves from morning to night are potentially nothing to us. If we died, they would dissolve in our tightest grasp, forgotten if they were in our mind, lost if they were in our hand, faded into blank numbness if they were our mind and body. Surprisingly, once we become accustomed to the omnipresent possibility of death in life, we feel greatly liberated. We realize we are essentially free at all times in all situations.*

We seek to penetrate linguistic, mythical, and religious depths in order that we may rejoin the eternal. We struggle with concepts such as formlessness, beyond, infinite space, final ultimacy, becoming one with the absolute, each one indefinable. The exhilarating freedom comes only from being dissolved in the eternal.

WE EVOLVED TO DIE: AWARENESS OF AWARENESS

Ed's anxiety about his impending death was compounded by his awareness. He said, "I know three things: one, that I'll be dying soon; two, I am not dead yet; and three, I can't stand the interval. Now I understand better your Myshkin story; he just wanted to get it over with." Ed was still missing the essence of the story: treasuring the experience of living and dying. Not only was he aware that he was dying, that the whole thing was unfamiliar, that he was losing himself and everything dear to him, and that he was a coward and greedy but, even more significant, he was aware of his awareness of all these things. This awareness of his awareness had turned into such a discouraging fury that he could no longer maintain his dignity.

Never mind the awareness of such a serious matter as dying, even awareness of the ordinary acts and habits interferes with their experience. There is a story of a man with a long beard who, after being asked whether in bed he keeps his beard over or under the cover, can no longer sleep.

Awareness of our existence is the ultimate reward and punishment for our evolution. Animals are aware of their environment and their enemies but not aware of their awareness. They communicate with each other within their species and perhaps even across species. They are instinctively aware of and act on their physiological impulses: hunger, fighting, coupling, protecting offspring, and the like.

Humans share this physiological awareness. However, in the evolutionary process, we developed an additional awareness, of these awarenesses. For example, not only do we get hungry and look for food but we know, that we are hungry and that we are looking for food. Primitive awareness of sexuality must exist in animals, at least to recognize their reproductive partners, and they have an instinctual drive to reproduce, as we do. However, we are also cognitively aware that if we do not reproduce, our genes will not be passed on to the next generation.

It is interesting that the same evolutionary process condemns us to dying—we die because we reproduce sexually. Those organisms that reside at the bottom of the evolutionary chain merely clone; they do not reproduce sexually. Once they bud, the genetic makeup remains forevermore. In fact, they never die unless they are directly destroyed. But they never experience what we would consider aging or natural death. Only when an organism gets high enough in the evolutionary chain does sexual reproduction occur, and when it does it is always accompanied by natural aging and eventual death. Therefore, one may look at death as an evolutionary phenomenon. And we are still evolving in nature. At some time in the future, we may yet evolve to something else that our present awareness cannot capture.

The cognitive awareness of dying is like any other awareness of awareness. That I will disappear and the rest will remain is a recognition of one's being a separate entity. That sense of separateness is the source of dread of death—the ultimate disruption of one's sense of continuity. The serenity of dying, by contrast, comes from sensing our nonseparateness and believing in our destiny, which is ultimately being one with nature, from which we all came.

The very process of thinking separates us from endless existence. As long as we are conscious of our separateness, we are not experiencing the moment of being part of the eternal universe. The actual experience of the moment, not the thought of it, is the closest one can get to eternity. Immortality is then experienced as a present fact. In the repetitive words of the Tantric aphorism, "It is here! It is here!"

FROM HERE TO NOTHINGNESS

I am interested in what remains
after the pot is broken.

—Mary Caroline Richards

"I wish I were a fervent believer in the afterlife, as my wife is," said Ed. "She has such a hopeful outlook about her death.

For her, it means eternity. Of course, she isn't exactly dying either. I tried, but just couldn't do it. So, now I have nothing to look forward to. The word *nothing* is frightening by itself. Here, I am someone, I have some relationship, some external things. I have a job, a title, an office, I have a telephone number belonging only to me. I have credit cards in my name. Newspapers and magazines are delivered to my address. These are all part of me. It isn't totally true to say that they define me, but to some extent they do. Of course, I also have my ideas, my thoughts, my feelings. How could I become 'a nothing'? Incidentally, is it 'a nothing' or just 'nothing'? You said the other day: 'We ought to think of everything as if it were on loan to us.' Does that include our bodies and our minds?" The answer is yes.

"Nothingness" is disorganizing to even the most stable minds. There is a sense of the basic fragility of human life and of the solitary and unsheltered condition of the individual confronted with the threat of nothingness. That single, pervasive sense of finitude embraces humanity enough to give one the chills.

Thoughts of eternity are the bright side of our ending in this world. Its realm and its nature change from one culture to another, from one religion to another, but there is always a colorful and generous destination. It is being forever, happily. The foreboding of death, by contrast, is the dark side of our ending, an oblivion; nothingness.

It is virtually impossible to conceptualize the nothing if one uses external factors as a point of reference, because "nothing" isn't a "something." "Nothing is simply nothing." Something external involves a space, is defined by shape, location, and boundaries. Its presence has an effect. But nothing cannot have effect. It cannot be a thing, a realm, a state, or a place. This ultimate end is the diametric opposite of everything external, like all Ed's explanatory props. The Sufis' way to the universal self meant removing the veils of external life one at a time until they ultimately attained the final state—nothingness. A popular tale told by A. R. Arestah and K. S. Sheikh expresses this state.

> At one of the great court banquets, where everyone sat according to his rank . . . , a shabbily dressed man entered the hall and took a seat above everyone else. [When asked to identify himself], the stranger replied that he ranked above [the king]. "Then you must be the Prophet," declared the prime minister. The visitor claimed that he outranked [them all]. The prime minister shouted angrily, "Are you then God?" The man calmly replied, "I am above that too!" Contemptuously the prime minister asserted, "There is nothing above God." [To this the man finally succumbed and said], "Now you know my identity. That nothing is me."

The path of the Sufi toward an eternal self also means the elimination of all labels, knowledge, and concepts in order to achieve not a nothingness but its opposite, an *everythingness,* because only nothing is everything.

ONLY IN DEATH—IN PRIMORDIAL DISSOLUTION— DOES ONE FIND THE ETERNAL LIFE

The universe is timeless. Eternity, like space, is nonlinear. Our awareness is a cross-sectional moment in a stream of ongoing existence. That stream cannot be divided into past, present, and future; it can only be experienced in the present as is. Therefore the self is no more than the experience of the instant on an apparent continuity. Our body, mind, and soul and everything else are perpetually present in such nonlinear existence.

Gary Zukav in *The Seat of the Soul* writes, "Consider the ocean. Now reach in and grab a cup full of water. In that instant, the cup becomes individual, but it has always been, has it not? This is the case with your soul. There was the instant when you became a cup of energy, but it was of an immortal original Being."

When you empty the cup back into the ocean, the individuality of that entity disappears while always maintaining its potential, although the water that once occupied the cup will no longer remember its container when it merges with the ocean. One day another cup may scoop some water from this ocean of oblivion, and a new soul will be formed, unaware of its spiritual whole. James Hillman's book *The Soul's Code* tells a version of the legend of this oblivion in transformation. (It is in Book VI of the *Aeneid* that Virgil speaks of the souls being washed in the river Lethe and hung up to dry.)

> *Before the souls enter human life . . . they pass through the plain of Lethe [oblivion, forgetting] so that on arrival here all of the previous activities . . . [are] wiped out. It is in this condition of a tabula rasa, or empty tablet, that we are born. We have forgotten all of the story, though the inescapable and necessary pattern of [one's] lot remains.*

According to a Jewish legend, the evidence for this forgetting of the soul['s] prenatal election is pressed right into your upper lip. That little crevice below your nose is where the angel pressed its forefinger to seal your lips. That little indentation is all that is left to remind you of your preexistent soul life and so, as we conjure up an instant or a lost thought, our fingers go to that significant dent.

So, why do we not self-perpetuate? We do! Physically and spiritually. We just forgot.

THE WAY OF GOD IS BELIEVING AND LOVING

———◆———

SECULAR APOSTLE

BELIEVING IN GOD:
BELIEVING IN SOMETHING GREATER
THAN THE HUMAN DIMENSION

BELIEVING IN THE EXISTENCE OF GOD
IN THE FORM OF ABSENCE

THE LOVE OF GOD

THE LOVE OF DIVINE LAW

One cannot rest on one's soulful and spiritual laurels.

SECULAR APOSTLE

Secular spirituality has outstripped its conceptual basis, as astronomical observation once outstripped Ptolemaic cosmology, ultimately resulting in the Copernican revolution. A breakthrough in the spiritual arena can be made possible only by a backward leap, returning to faith, that is, believing in and loving God.

The person who loves others, his or her work and belonging, who believes in the sacredness of everything, unity and transformation, may try to live a soulful and spiritual life. But how does a person gain and cultivate these extraordinary tenets, and where does he or she get the energy and the inspiration to maintain such an existence? The answer is: believing in and loving God. Secular apostles bring to others a philosophy of life that only they themselves may be able to uphold. The rest, who need and search for additional help from other secular institutions, such as philosophy, science, and therapy, end up getting more weight rather than weight-bearing support. In fact, all these institutions themselves deplete their source of energy by negating, explaining, or interpreting God. One who believes in God, by contrast, is eternally fueled by His divine energy.

In *Who Needs God,* Rabbi Harold Kushner asks, "What is

the difference between a person who relies only on himself and a person who has learned to turn to God for help?" He replies that it is not that one will do bad things while the other will do good things. In fact, the self-reliant atheist may be a fine, upstanding person. "The difference is," he replies, that "the atheist is like a bush in the desert." What this means is, if he has only himself to rely on, then when he exhausts his internal resources, he is at the risk of running dry and withering. However, the man or woman who turns to God is "like a tree planted by a stream"; what such people share with the world is replenished from a source beyond themselves, so they never run dry.

Secular spiritualists tend to consider God an unnecessary burden, wishing Him away. On the contrary, God brings no burden. In fact, it is said that humanity and God are like a bird and its wings. Imagine if a bird were unaware that its wings enabled it to fly; the wings would only add an extra burden of weight.

The belief in God is the transcendence of self, as it is the source of faith and humility. The love of God is the eternal verity, as it is the source of enlightenment and peacefulness. Together they bring to humanity the ultimate happiness: joyful serenity.

BELIEVING IN GOD: BELIEVING IN SOMETHING GREATER THAN THE HUMAN DIMENSION

Two questions are frequently asked: Is there a God? If so, what is God? In keeping with the philosopher Karl Jaspers, you may say, "There is no God, for there is only the world, and the world is God." Or in synchrony with Immanuel Kant, you may be awed by the enormity of a starry night, in which time and space seem to become interchangeable, forming a spectacular tapestry. There you realize that the earth is only one minute portion of the mystic galaxy; you pause and exclaim, "Ah, there must be God!" Such a moment reflects the realization of the sheer wonder and beauty of existence—a seashell, a leaf, a bird's nest—and partakes of God's mystery. If you believe in skies even without remotely comprehending them, you automatically believe in God.

Even closer to home, you cannot help being awed by the complexity of your own body: your heart beats without any effort on your part, and you breathe without your own awareness. A myriad of hormones, neurotransmitters, and other messenger molecules pass through a perfectly programmed system. All of this represents the visible programming of the world, the universe, and our bodies. Then you wonder: "How could that be? Is there a programmer in all of this? Is the programmer God?"

Anybody who reflects on such events and experiences soon realizes that there is an intangible dimension of the universe, often referred to as mystical or spiritual or cosmic, which is not readily available to one's senses. All these questions about God are difficult to answer unless one concedes the existence of another reality radically different from the one we commonly experience. If one is convinced that there is something much greater than the human dimension, one is a believer, says Deepak Chopra.

GOD HAS EVOLVED WITH US

The evolution of human beings began with the evolution of our minds and our attempts to understand the external world. Whatever we couldn't make sense of, we attributed to supernatural forces. These forces evolved from the most primitive gods to highly organized religions, only to be challenged with the evolving mind's reasoning.

Our attitude toward God has perhaps found greatest expression in some Old Testament injunctions, such as "Thou shalt not make unto thee any graven image or likeness." This initially meant that, because God is invisible, we must not worship Him in statues, idols, or effigies. Not simply a tangible prohibition, this injunction soon developed into the metaphorical idea that God is not only invisible but also inconceivable, unthinkable. Neither symbol nor metaphor can describe Him and, furthermore, none may take His place. When we say something like "He is uninferable, unimaginable, indescribable," we are still using human language and

concepts of a finite human being. Even the word *He* betrays
its humanly conceived core. As Karl Jaspers tells us in *Way to
Wisdom,* "All metaphorical representations of God without
exception are myths, meaningful as such when understood to
be mere hints and parallels, but they become superstitions
when mistaken for the reality of God Himself. Since every
image conceals as much as it discloses, we come closest to God
in the negation of images."

Even though the images are negated, the symbols and
metaphors avoided, and visualization, thinking, and conceiv-
ing all prohibited, we cannot help attributing certain human
qualities to God. This is because human beings understand
by personifying. The Book of Genesis says that God created
Adam in his own image, but we keep reversing the process.
In *A History of God,* a history of Judaism, Christianity, and
Islam, Karen Armstrong notes a central motif in these three
Abrahamic religions: a personal meeting between God and
man, wherein God relates by means of a dialogue. We are
adamant in overly personalizing God, whom we insist must
talk to us in the way that humans talk rather than in more
enigmatic ways. As Armstrong says, " . . . rabbis, priests, and
Sufis [should] have warned me not to expect to experience
[God] as an objective fact that could be discovered by the
ordinary process of rational thought. They would have told
me that . . . God was a product of the creative imagination,
like . . . poetry and music."

During the Enlightenment, liberal Judeo-Christian the-
ologians increasingly moved away from the notion of God as
a literal person. That depersonalization of God has continued
into the modern day. The conceptualization of God-as-
person, though not meaningful, may be useful, if not
inevitable, for some people. Each individual, if not each soci-

ety, finds its God in idiosyncratic ways, frequently determined by its developmental stage. The Renaissance thinker Giovanni Pico della Mirandola said, "We have made thee neither of heaven nor of earth, neither mortal nor immortal, so that with freedom of choice and with honor, as thou the maker and molder of thyself thou mayest fashion thyself in whatever shape thou shalt prefer."

It is interesting that, with such freedom to choose the shape and design, including that of a bearded old man with a not very pleasant temperament, we all have established God's sameness:

There is One Ultimate Being, the Ground of all existence.

The Divine Essence is unknowable.

God is both immanent, in the sense that He appears in all phenomenal forms, and transcendent, in the sense that He is the Absolute Reality above and beyond every appearance.

While the forms of the universe change and pass and are simultaneously renewed without a moment's intermission, the essence of the universe is coeternal with God.

WE ARE WIRED FOR GOD

I believe, therefore I am.

Whether it is a *koan* that we try to decipher (as in Zen Buddhism) or a treasure that we try to discover (as in Sufism), or a biblical figure that we try to emulate (as in Christianity), in many other ways we attempt to understand our relation to a greater force.

In his novel *One Hundred Years of Solitude,* the Colombian

author Gabriel García Márquez tells of a village where people are afflicted with a strange plague of forgetfulness, a kind of contagious amnesia that keeps working its way through the entire population. One young man, still unaffected, attempts to prevent the damage by putting labels on everyday objects and events, such as "This is a table," "This is a cow that has to be milked every morning." At the entrance to the town, on the main road, he put up two large signs: One reads, "The name of our village is Macondo," and an even larger one reads, "God exists."

We are born with the knowledge of God. God is an imprinted knowledge that can be forbidden or denied, but it cannot be erased. Look what happened in the Soviet Union after seventy years of suppression of religion. It seems the moment Communism collapsed, worshiping God returned in full force. Ana-Maria Rizzuto's psychoanalytic study *The Birth of the Living God* is confirmatory:

> *One patient among those I have studied, the daughter of militantly atheistic parents, reported locking her door at the age of seven, kneeling on the floor, and praying for a long time, "Please let there be a God." While she was praying she felt guilty of betraying her parents and afraid of being found kneeling, but her need for worshiping somebody, something was stronger than their prohibition.*

Human beings are innately spiritual beings. We may need to worship as soon as we become aware of ourselves. Around the age of four, children begin to ask the why of everything. A child may ask who moves the clouds and why. If told "the wind," she will not be satisfied but will want to know who moves the wind. Similarly, when she becomes curious about babies and how they are made, and is told that babies are made by "mommies and daddies in Mommy's tummy," the child still wants to know. It is this ceaseless chaining of questions that inevitably ends in the answer "God" does these things! Often that notion suffices for the child's inner need, even if she asks, "What is God?"

An extraordinary example of the deep desire to believe in God is cited by Karen Armstrong in her book *A History of God*. She tells the story of a group of Jewish concentration camp victims who decide one day to create a mock trial in which God is brought up on charges of extreme cruelty and betrayal. Despite arguments for and against God, the members of this impromptu court collectively find no evidence of His Divine intervention as a benevolent Being who counters evil and answers the prayers of good people. In fact, nothing dispels their fervent sense in His absolute and inexcusable culpability. They have no choice but to condemn Him. The rabbi of the group announces the final verdict: God is guilty as charged and should be punished with the death penalty. Shortly thereafter, however, the rabbi glances up at those assembled, says that the trial has concluded, and announces, "It is time for the evening prayer."

IF YOU DOUBT, YOU ARE A BELIEVER

You may encounter people who are nonbelievers, or who are at best skeptical of God's existence. But that very skepticism is the first indication that one believes in *something*. That something usually turns out to be God. This fact confirms the renowned theologian Paul Tillich's paradoxical point in his book *Man's Right to Knowledge*: If you start with the assertion that God exists, you can reach Him less than if you assert that He doesn't exist. In every culture without exception, every human being, including the atheist, sooner or later—especially at times of the impending loss of a loved one or one's own severe illness or dying—longs for God. Could this yearning be a passion welling up from our deepest instinctual forces? Even Lynne Cox, a confirmed unbeliever, tells how she succumbed to such a force as she visited the old city of Jerusalem in her charming anecdote "To Aqaba":

> *Late afternoon. I am standing above the Western Wall, also known as the Wailing Wall, in the old section of Jerusalem. All the cracks [in the wall] are filled with paper. Some are brittle and yellow, some are mere fragments, and some are on air mail envelopes and hotel stationery. I could see a few with words exposed: there was one in French, others in German and Hebrew and Russian and English. I wondered what these prayers were all about. Were they praying for someone who was ill, for friends, for family, for peace or prosperity? What were their hopes and their dreams? Did they really believe they could get a message to God through this wall? Every single crack in the wall to my right and left, above my head and beside my feet was filled with paper. I kept looking. Three meters above my head was a hole the size of a tennis ball. I crumpled my note up into a tight wad, looked around, hoping that no one was watching. I leaned back and tossed my message up.*

BELIEVING IN THE EXISTENCE OF GOD IN THE FORM OF ABSENCE

> *When someone quotes the old poetic image about clouds*
> *gradually uncovering the moon, slowly loosen knot*
> *by knot the strings of your robe.*
> *Like this?*
> *If anyone wonders how Jesus raised the dead,*
> *don't try to explain the miracle.*
> *Kiss me on the lips.*
> *Like this. Like this.*

> —Jalālu'l-Dīn Rūmi

FAITH IS BELIEVING THE UNBELIEVABLE

The mind experiences the world with the five senses of the body and lives and generates values and judgments based on this touchable, hearable, tasteable, smellable, and seeable realm. In the Gospel of Thomas, Jesus says that his role in life is to point the disciples away from the rule of these five senses:

> *I shall give you what no eye has seen and what no ear has heard*
> *and what no hand has touched and what has never occurred to*
> *the human mind.*

What lies beyond scientific discourse based on five senses and one mind? It is a power outside the province of science, beyond the grasp of the human mind, a power that can subsume everything. Those who endow researchers with the sole source of truth are forfeiting that power. Scientists are limited by their scientific role. After all, they are asked only to collect data on certain subjects and to build hypotheses to explain them. Yet the database they are willing to explore can, at its best, represent only part of reality. Scientific research is typically not designed to examine all of the wondrous and intangible forms of human experience. Science can only accept what it can validate. It cannot explain everything. The illusive idea of God, in contrast, has the extraordinary capacity to explain everything: it encompasses not merely measurable phenomena but phenomena personally felt and subliminally sensed, which can even include revelations that can be communicated only through spiritual or mystical channels. Unlike science, the concept of God extends beyond the scientists' tangible world.

One cannot find God with the mind's reason. Trusting contemplation brings us to Him. When I read the following anecdote, as told by Noah benShea, I shivered:

A man is driving his car too fast down a treacherous mountain pass. The car goes over the cliff, and the man barely survives by reaching out and grabbing a clump of bushes growing from the side of the mountain wall. Dangling in space, the man pleads with God: "Please, help me. Rescue me. I will change forever. I will do anything. Please. Help me."

God calls out to the man, "You want my help?"

"Yes," says the man. "Anything. Anything!"

"I'll help you on one condition," says the voice of God.

"Anything."

"All right," says God. "Trust me and let go."

Faith requires no understanding; in fact, it is undermined by such efforts. Faith needs just devoted and trusting believers; it needs steady allegiance and fidelity. Faith is spawned not by knowing but by unknowing. The knowledge of God is no knowledge. It is a mystical experience.

THE PHYSICAL ABSENCE OF GOD
IS THE PROOF OF HIS EXISTENCE

In the realm of stars, the light from the remotest stars is received last, and until the moment it arrives human beings *deny* that the stars are there. We can ask, "How many centuries does a spirit require to be comprehended?" Paraphrasing Isaac Newton, we are like children playing on the seashore. Now and then we find a smoother pebble or prettier shell than the ordinary, while the great ocean and what lies in it remain undiscovered to us. No child can comprehend that great ocean, the galaxies and beyond, and all the contradictory scientific explanations of how all that happened. The Big Bang for the child is exactly what it is: a bang. Not that it means a great deal more for the rest of us adults.

All religions contain contradictions and assertions that are impossible, which is in fact the very essence of religion. As witness to this, we repeat Tertullian's avowal: "And the Son of God is dead, which is worthy of belief because it is absurd. And when buried He rose again, which is certain because it is impossible."

God is a visible thing not by Himself but by His creation, the same way that atoms are not "things" in their atomic form but a large number of them put together suddenly become visible and recognizable objects.

All things and beings of the universe are the effects of a ubiquitous power from which they rise, which supports and sustains them during the period of their manifestation—and to which they must ultimately return. This attribution of power to an unknown and unknowable force is belief in God.

The light that sustains us here on earth comes from elsewhere, from the sun and the moon. Yet they are not on the earth; the presence of God is like rays of sun. He is on the earth and not on the earth; we know His existence only by His effects across the vast distances.

God is present to us in the form of such *absence*. As Simone Weil said, "The apparent absence of God in this world is the actual reality of God."

PRAYER: THE SOUL SPEECH

Now, there is a law written in the darkest of the Books of Life, and it is this: If you look at a thing nine hundred and ninety-nine times, you are perfectly safe; if you look at it the thousandth time, you are in frightful danger of seeing it for the first time.

—G. K. Chesterton

In his book *Poetry and Mysticism,* Colin Wilson describes the mystical experience as perhaps deceptively simple: like drawing aside a curtain or turning on a light switch. He then goes on to warn us that if we blunder into a completely dark room, we may feel the walls for hours before we find the switch. He concludes with an important proviso: Turning on the light is simple—when you know where the switch is! The curtain and switches are placed in different parts of the room in different houses. Yet they are still curtains and switches serving the same light.

One of the common paths to finding the switch is prayer. Although different religions seem to have their own rituals of prayer—Christians bow their heads and fold their hands, Native Americans dance, Sufis whirl, Buddhists sit quietly, and Orthodox Jews move their torsos back and forth saying ritualized words aloud—they all serve to send the person in the direction of the switch.

Words of prayer in all religions are similar: praising God, asking for mercy and forgiveness, declaring loyalty and obedience, asking for peace, appealing to God's will and compassion. They tend to be repetitive and harmonious, with variations on a theme. In his recent book *How to Know God,* Deepak Chopra says 99 percent of a spiritual journey is repetition. In any other form of communication, this pattern could be banal and boring. In praying and recitation of mantras, however, one feels a stillness of mind—a tender composure—one's mantra may even be one's personal name for God.

There is a positive correlation between the amount of time one spends in prayer and one's ability to remain faithful. God will receive all your prayers and never be tired of hearing you, says Rabbi Harold Kushner.

He tells the Hasidic story of the tailor who came to his rabbi and said, "I have a problem with my prayers. If someone came to me and said, 'Mendel, you're a wonderful tailor,' that would make me feel good. I'd feel appreciated. I would go on feeling good for a whole week, even longer, on the strength of just a single compliment like that. But if they came to me every day, one after another, hour after hour, and kept repeating to me, 'Mendel, you're a wonderful tailor, Mendel, you're a wonderful tailor,' over and over again, it would really drive me crazy, so much so that I wouldn't want to listen to them anymore. I would undoubtedly tell them to simply go away and leave me in peace. In fact, that is what bothers me about prayer. I would think that if God were told how wonderful He was once a week or every few weeks, and only a few of us at a time, what more would He want? After all, is God so insecure that He needs us praising him morning, noon, and night? And does everyone have to praise Him? It seems to me that would drive Him crazy, too."

The rabbi smiled at Mendel and replied, "You're absolutely right. You have no idea how difficult it is for God to listen to all of our praises, hour after hour, day after day. But it is only because God knows how important it is for us to utter that praise. Because of His great love for us, He tolerates all of our prayers, no matter how many."

MAN FINDS GOD IN HIS OWN GOD-LIKE BEHAVIOR

When I know who I am, like Mother Teresa, I'll have no problem in knowing what to do.

—Charlotte Joko Beck

Prayer is a longing to encounter God, but frequently it degenerates from silent communion to a selfish seeking of God's favor and turns meditation into an invocation of Him for personal, self-serving purposes. God always answers our prayers, but when we use prayer in this way, His answer is usually No!

In prayer, we are to seek not practical gain but rather spiritual gain—the discovery of our divinity. We have to contemplate and to know what we have to become to achieve it, not wish that it be granted. Jesus can be regarded either as one who, by the nature of austerities and meditation, attained wisdom or as God's enactment of a human career. The former view would lead one to imitate the master literally, to find the transcendent, redemptive experience. The latter view provides a symbol of the hero to be contemplated, rather than an example to be followed.

Since the Divine Being is a revelation of the ultimate Self that dwells within us all, communion with God should be undertaken as a meditation on one's own immanent divinity, not as of literal imitation. If God meets you only from without and not from within, then you have God outside and not in your soul. Sometimes Christ has been imitated without the imitator coming anywhere near the ideal or its meaning; superficial and false believers have turned God into an external object of worship. But it is this very veneration of the object that prevents us from reaching into the depths of our soul and transforming it into a deeply spiritual wholeness. If God remains an external image, we remain untouched within the deepest part of ourselves. Happy, says Louis Pasteur, is he who bears God within.

Even a good-faith imitation of God changes a man, and may slowly prepare him for true wholeness. In either case, the genuine experience of God is always a slow process. As Zen Master Shunryu Suzuki tells us:

Even though you try very hard, the progress you make is always little by little. It is not like going out in a shower in which you know when you get wet. It is more like being in a fog, you do not know you are getting wet, but as you keep walking you get wet little by little.

When God is sought with such selfless perseverance, His answer is always Yes!

THE LOVE OF GOD

Only love with no object brings peacefulness.

THE DIVINE KNOWLEDGE
IS UNLEARNED LEARNING

*Enlightenment is not something you achieve, it
is the absence of something.*

—Charlotte Joko Beck

Learned learning may generate a sense of "knowledge," leading to isolation and lack of inner sustainment. Of course, we
know that in the Book of Genesis, eating the fruit of the tree
of knowledge is represented as a deadly sin. Even in ancient
times, it was believed that in knowledge the gods are robbed
of their fire.

Yūnus Emre, the famed Sufi poet, also doubtful of knowledge, praised only unlearned learning. He along with several
other saints and holy men had the reputation of being illiterate. This reputation made their achievement seem even
greater to the common folk and enabled him to share a char-
acteristic with Muhammad, the Prophet, who was also a
"self-proclaimed illiterate." This concept of the simple holy

man untainted by worldly learning is common to all religious traditions. Emre himself spoke disparagingly of *ilm* (formal book learning), which he compared unfavorably with *irfān* (soulful knowledge). "Holy ignorance . . . verges on the sacred," says Thomas Moore in *Original Self.*

DIVINE KNOWLEDGE IS THE INNER BIRTH OF THE MESSIAH

"Who is there?" asks God.
"It is I."
"Go away," God says. . . .
Later . . .
"Who is there?" asks God.
"It is Thou."
"Enter," replies God.

—Charlotte Joko Beck

The Hindu saying "None but a god can worship God," is intended not to be blasphemy but to urge us to dissolve into a godlike existence of our own. The love of God takes away "I"-ness. For the same reason, Christ is conceived as a bridge (the Pope, vicar of Christ, is still called the pontiff, from *pons,* meaning "bridge"). So the Incarnation represents the presence of the invisible in the common matter of human life. Thus, a god-man, who is both visible and invisible, becomes joined into one. Jesus is both a divinely inspired but visible man and the invisible God borrowing human shape. Duality transcended; forms disappear and all elemental forces embody themselves in a human being and reconcile humankind with God.

Why should I seek? I am the same as he.
His essence speaks through me.
I have been looking for myself!

—Jalālu'l-Dīn Rūmi

Yūnus Emre pleaded with God for such union when he said, "Give me a love so that I won't know where I am. Let me lose myself; seeking, let me not find myself. Take away, remove from me 'I-ness'; fill me with 'You-ness.' Kill me in Your Life, so that I won't go there and die." For centuries, stories and legends end in parting from this world and divine dissolution. In Japanese tales, the hero frequently is left in the same position at the end that he occupied in the beginning, except that he has become one with his mission. Similarly, American cowboys, at the end of their heroic deeds, ride off alone into the dissolving sunset.

In his writings on deification, the great thirteenth-century mystic poet Jalālu'l-Dīn Rūmi speaks of the phrase *Ana 'l-Haqq*, "I am God." Although it may seem that such words make a presumptuous claim, it is really even more presumptuous to say *Ana 'l-'abd*, "I am the slave of God." It is the former that is actually an expression of great humility. The reason is as follows: The person who says "I am the slave of God" affirms two existences, his own and God's, but the person who says, "I am God," has made himself nonexistent. He has given himself up by virtue of those words, in effect reducing himself in relation to God and believing "I am naught. He is all: there is no being but God's."

Thus the person arrived, transformed, relies on the message and not on the messenger, the content of the teaching, not the teacher; and the laws, not the judge. Although the Gospel according to St. Mark, says that the disciples thought of Jesus as their appointed king, the apocryphal Gospel of Thomas affirms otherwise when it presents the following story:

> Jesus said to his disciples, "Compare me to someone and tell me whom I am like." Simon Peter said to him, "You are like a righteous angel." Matthew said to him, "You are like a wise philosopher." Thomas said to him, "Master, my mouth is wholly incapable of saying whom you are like." Jesus said, "I am not your master. Because you have drunk, you have become drunk from the bubbling stream which I have measured out."

A well-known Zen story tells of a student being taught to meditate on his breath.

> One day the student rushed to his master saying that he had seen the images of Buddha, radiating light. Ah, yes, said the master, but don't worry; if you keep your mind on the breath, they will go away.

If we keep our minds on the message of God, we need not seek His concrete presence.

That is why Rabbi Harold Schulweis of Los Angeles, who coined the term *predicate theology,* says when you find statements about God—for example, "God is love," "God is truth"—concentrate on the *predicate*—love, truth—instead of the subject. "God is about love, truth, caring, kindness, compassion, charity, and humility."

THE LOVE OF DIVINE LAW

THE DIVINE LAW REQUIRES SELF-JUDGMENT

Knock on your inner door and no other.

—Jalālu'l-Dīn Rūmi

The Unitarian minister G. Peter Fleck recalls a drama on television:

> *A man dies and he then finds himself standing on line, upon which an usher appears and tells him that he can choose either door—the one on the right leading to heaven, the one on the left leading to hell. The man immediately asked in a querulous voice, "You mean I can choose either one? And there is no judgment, no taking account of how I lived?" "That's right," the usher replied. Then, in an irritated tone, he ordered the man to move along, saying, "People are dying and lining up behind you. Choose one door and keep the line moving!" But, the man was still unsettled, and said, "I want to confess; I want to come clean; I want to be judged." The usher in turn replied, "We don't have time for that. Just choose a door and move along!"*

The man chose to walk through the door on the left, leading to hell. What moral can we take from this story? Fleck's conclusion is that, in the end, we all want to be held accountable. We want to be judged.

Though we need the judgment of our fellow human beings, we all defer to God for the final judgment, which is not directly available. With forthright self-awareness and honesty in both self-accusation and self-affirmation, we can indirectly find God's judgment.

Religions, under the umbrella term *sin,* provide broad-based guidelines for such self-judgment. Sin is considered transgression of Divine law, a willful violation of its principles. All religions have essentially the same formulation of what is sinful: pride, envy, avarice, sloth, wrath, gluttony, and lust. Every religion provides a punishment to the sinner, even if in the form of forgiveness.

Even in the most forgiving religion, such as Buddhism, wherein there is no damnation, there is still karmic retribution. Although karmic retribution of bad behaviors isn't considered a punishment, it has justice as its natural consequence, similar to the concept of Judeo-Christian religion that one reaps only what one has sown. If you throw a stone to hurt someone else, it will fall back down on your own head. Whoever digs a pit may fall into it. If this dynamic is so clear and obvious, why do some people keep sinning? It is not because some people are good, others bad, but because they are not fully grown-up yet.

The sinner's mind is that of a very young child—a dual mind that wants simply to have its cake and eat it too. The child is responsible and irresponsible, rational and irrational, predictable and not, without realizing such duality. The equanimity of adulthood requires one to transcend the dual mode of thinking of childhood. In fact, the very word *transcend* means to go past that duality.

All religions, East and West, exhort the individual, in unusual unison, to decenter, to loosen his ego-oriented boundaries and follow the path to transcend himself. For most people, such exhortation remains an unattainable ideal—a lofty goal, an abstract idea that only makes them feel more inadequate, and more hopeless. This is because the transcendence of the self requires, first, becoming adult. In fact, some of the problems they are experiencing have less to do with failure of transcending than with failure of obtaining adulthood. As M. Scott Peck tells us in his *Road Less Traveled,* "The path to sainthood goes through adulthood. There are no quick and easy shortcuts. Ego boundaries must be hardened before they can be softened. An identity must be established before it can be transcended. One must find one's self before one can lose it."

THE DIVINE LAW REQUIRES
THE PERFECT REPENTANCE

Cast your sins upon yourself.

Every religion demands from the sinner recognition of sin, feelings of guilt, and expression of both. Christ appears to have regarded sinners as being closest to the perfection of humanity, and he saw sinners' transformational potential. He saw sin and suffering as themselves holy things, indeed modes of perfection. The rationale here is that sainthood can derive from the depths of sinfulness and sufferings, as long as every sin is followed by confession and contrition. (*Contritio* is "perfect" repentance and *attritio* "imperfect" repentance.

The former sees sin as the potential to reach the highest goodness; the latter is primarily driven by the fear of punishment.)

The perfect repentance means:

Taking on full responsibility for one's own sin. Full responsibility for one's sins is not the superficial understanding that because Christ took upon himself the sins of the world, we can conveniently cast our sins upon Him and walk away.

Full confession. We must look upon our sin with abhorrence, admit to it, and make a break with the past.

Full compensation to the harmed. Not only must we take complete responsibility for our sin but our *contritio* must extend beyond feelings to actions, undoing the harm generated by the sin. According to Sufi legend (as told by James Carse), Abu Yazid made his periodic journey to purchase supplies at the bazaar in Hamadhan, for which he traveled several hundred miles. When he returned home, he discovered a colony of ants in his cardamom seeds. He carefully packed the seeds up again and walked back across the desert to the merchant from whom he had bought them. His intent was not to exchange the seeds but to return the ants to their home.

For some people sinning becomes a bad habit, if not an entrenched addiction. They transgress, violate the most precious relationships, and still expect understanding and forgiveness. Whether at work, in the family, or in the community, they frequently fail in their commitments and shortchange their responsibilities, and still wait for charitable responses. God may forgive you indefinitely, but that doesn't mean you should keep sinning and demanding forgiveness forever. One would think, it is enough to taste one drop of the sea to know that it is salty, as the old expression goes. But some people do not stop; they keep drinking until they get salt poisoning.

If you don't know when to stop sinning, at least you must know when to stop asking for forgiveness. It is the child within us who expects the world to behave toward us like the mother who never really was. Somehow, no matter how bad we were, our mother was supposed to accept and love us unconditionally, forgive all our mischiefs and undesirable feelings. This was never true when we were children, nor should it have been, and it is definitely not applicable to adult relationships. No spouse should keep forgiving repetitive affairs, no boss should tolerate chronic lateness, no friend should appreciate lack of reciprocation. Even Abraham knew when to stop asking for forgiveness from God.

In the Book of Genesis, when the Lord considered punishing the entire cities of Sodom and Gomorrah because of their serious sins, Abraham recognized that there must have been some innocent people in the cities as well. He asked, "Are you really going to sweep away the innocent with the guilty? What if there are fifty innocent people in the city? It would be unthinkable for you to do such a thing, to treat the innocent and the guilty alike and to kill the innocent with the guilty. Won't the judge of the whole earth do what is fair?" The Lord said, "If I find fifty innocent people inside the city of Sodom, I will spare the whole place for their sake." Then Abraham apologetically kept asking, what if there were only forty, or thirty, or twenty, or ten? The Lord repeated his promise: "I will not destroy it for the sake of the ten." But Abraham did not ask, "What if there are fewer than ten?"

The virtue of the sin is arriving at a stage where one does not need to sin. Only by such arrival has the purpose of the sin been obtained. For Christopher Lasch, in *Culture of Narcissism,* sin is to be valued because it sets the stage for spiritual cultivation by means of chastity, purity, charity, self-sacrifice, and ascetic surrender to the Holy. Ultimately, as he says, the reward of virtue is to have little to apologize for or to repent of at the end of one's life.

EPILOGUE

—◆—

UNTYING THE ENDS, FALLIBLY

Holidays, books and lives draw to their close.
The curtain rings down on some theater piece.
The brass, string, and percussion sections close
In on their tonic and concordant close.
When all loose ends infallibly are tied.

—Anthony Hecht

The Dalai Lama has said that human beings can do without religion, but they cannot do without love, compassion, and tenderness. For this reason, he makes a distinction between the religious and the spiritual. Being spiritual suggests developing those loving and caring human qualities, independent of any dogma, be it religious, political, or philosophical.

When he deemphasizes the importance of religion in contrast to spirituality, the Dalai Lama doesn't mean to negate God. On the contrary, he simply wants to distance himself from "designer" religions, or from rote practices devoid of holiness and, even more so, from not so innocuous zealotry—religionism. Wayne Oates, one of the founders of the pastoral counseling movement, spoke of this problem by telling the story of a young man who had gouged out one of his own eyes because Jesus said, "If your eye offends you, pluck it out." Of course, this kind of literalness was never intended in the scriptures, but concrete religiosity may promote such extreme acts. What is intended is *lectio divina,* a meditative reading of the scriptures. There are those who think they are religious because they mechanically practice all the rituals, although they remain not even remotely spiritual. As Frederic and Mary Ann Brussat observe in *Spiritual Literacy:*

> *People go to religious services and yet continue to pollute, take excessive profits, encourage wars, oppress, foment political division, maintain racial injustice, and promote their own moralistic agendas at the expense of a deeply moral responsiveness to a world in trouble.*

Such religionism frequently ends up superseding the intended spirituality of religions, by emphasizing theology and fundamentalism. For Martin Buber, true religion is experiencing God; the rest—theology—is talking about God. He goes on to say that the difference between them is the difference between having dinner and reading a menu.

Tribal prejudices are natural social phenomena; when religions are used to harden already existing tribal conflicts, the opposite of what the Divinity intended occurs. Over the centuries these tribalizations of religion have been perpetuated with even greater differentiation. Even within one sect, there are numerous subsects. America's increasing religious pluralism especially raises the specter of "McReligion," and its followers end up being "neither fish nor fowl nor good red herring," says Winifred Gallagher.

Out of these distortions and compromises, spirituality, the very purpose of religious divinity, has suffered. Every religion has an element of ritual piety. The original meaning of *ritual* (*ritus* in Latin) is correct action—not compulsion. If practiced in their intended spirit, rituals are holy actions. But if they preempt their intended purpose, they will prevent people from the immediacy of religious experience. In extreme determination, discipline makes one obsessed, not spiritual. Making the analogy to a ship at sea, John Gribbin says that a compass needle on a ship always points to the north magnetic pole, but that doesn't mean the ship is always sailing north. Devotional discipline can be a symptom of legalism, work righteousness, obsessive-compulsive neurosis or, worse, moralism.

Robert J. Ringer, in *Looking Out for Number One,* describes "the Absolute Moralist" as looking deceptively like any ordinary human being, who spends his life deciding what is right for *you*. If he gives to charity, he'll try to shame you into "understanding" that it's your moral duty to give to charity too (usually the charity of his choice). If he believes in Christ, he's certain that it's his moral duty to help you "see the light." In the most extreme case, he may even feel morally obliged to kill you in order to "save" you.

Although religion is primarily intended to serve the spiritual needs of its members, it has many other functions. One has to make an effort to distill the spiritual nature of religion without negating its procedures and ceremonies, and prejudices.

It has been said that a poet dares be just so clear and no clearer; he must approach lucid ground warily, like a mariner who is careful not to scrape the bottom of his boat on anything solid. Equally, secular spiritualists need to take distance from the apostate as much as they do from the anointed, and be careful about distilling God and spirituality from religion, for only religion can tie infallibly all the loose ends. As John O'Donohue says, the spirituality that cuts itself off from religion can go totally astray and become entangled in the worst forms of deception, illusion, and power. Cases in point are the horror stories of individuals subjected to insidious mind control by cults and sects that offer warmth and belonging—at the price of handing over one's mind. Since cults are reputedly adept at mind altering, they covertly, if not overtly, trap and exploit the natural longing for the spiritual, especially in vulnerable individuals.

Religion, in spite of its potential impediments, still provides the only direct, systematic, and cohesive articulation of humanity's relation to God. Spirituality, which lacks such cohesion, rests on the indirect support of religion, in the same way that music, having no adequate models, rests on the indirect support of two nonmusical aids—rhythm and words. Spirituality's teachings of love, compassion, work, belonging, believing in sanctity, unity, and transformation, and believing in and loving God, as well as variations on these themes, are all basic tenets of religion.

The basic teachings of the Western and Eastern religions, as civilizing forces, are indistinguishable. They all advocate honesty, kindness, faithfulness, loyalty, and the like. As we are told in the Vedas, "There is that one God they call by so many names."

One useful image of the common ground of all religions was presented by the Christian Bede Griffiths, who had spent most of his life in India. In a video interview made shortly before his recent death, he spread out his hand, saying religions are like separate fingers, quite distinct from each other. If you trace them to their source, however, you see that they all come together in the palm of your hand. Similarly, the thirteenth-century German mystic Meister Eckhart called God an underground river of wisdom with many wells tapping into it. All religions urge cultivation of spiritual depth: spirit in Christianity, life in Judaism, light in Islam, power in Taoism. They teach sacred existence, that spirituality is a measure of our humanity, and they all steer to deep waters and seek self-finding in order not to be self-centered.

All religions believe in the sacredness of the ordinary, like the rice hulling of Zen monks, the spinning of Gandhi, or the tent making of St. Paul. They all praise the feeling of oneness with the world, the wholeness in its primordial unity, and express the idea of holiness in nothingness. They urge us to seek the perfection inherent in ourselves: generosity, discipline, patience, diligence, love, and compassion. The religions may say to do "this" at least and be good, but ultimately they mean to know "it" and be God.

Religion is the natural ground of spirituality, a way of being in the world. For Winifred Gallagher, it is "the thread, running through human experience, that reminds our species of what's most important and real, yet so easily forgotten. Like memory, religion records the past, informs the present, and frames the future."

Most of us need a religion to believe in God; only within that context can we be soulful and spiritual, give meaning to our lives, and reach the ultimate happiness—joyful serenity. If this puzzles you, it is because it is what you already knew all along.

"We are spiritual beings on a human path, rather than human beings who may be on a spiritual path," as Jean Shinoda Bolen suggests. She continues: "Life is not only a journey but a pilgrimage . . . a quest for meaning, fulfillment, and wholeness." Humanity is a journey without a time and place of arrival. And we aren't alone. Near the end of her life, St. Teresa of Avila wrote, "The feeling remains that God is on the journey, too."

This faithful journey is difficult and arduous. There is no short path to a happy life. We know that the Jews wandered in the wilderness on the way to the Promised Land, just as Jesus of Nazareth took the long, arduous road to Jerusalem. Such homecoming from a secular exile is a humble occurrence. It may seem to be an extraordinarily ordinary event, or even no event. This is in keeping with Sam Keen's description: Bands will not play, the fatted calf won't be killed, a banquet need not be prepared, but there will be an innermost rejoicing as exile ends gradually, with no dramatic, external events to mark its passing. "The haze in the air evaporates and the world comes into focus; seeking gives way to finding; anxiety to satisfaction. Nothing is changed and everything is changed."

Well, this book also draws to its close. I hope, dear reader, in this journey, your world became a little better focused. You have to keep writing your own sonnets on the road. If you do, while nothing may seem to be changing for you, everything is changing and will continue to change, until you arrive. And when there, you'll find that you knew what you were seeking, in fact you had been there all along.

Now I must turn my lights off so that you can turn on your own and get home safely. I leave you with words from Noah benShea's *The Word:*

> *Once there was a student who was with a teacher for many years.*
> *And when the teacher felt he was going to die, he wanted to make*

even his death a lesson. That night, the teacher took a torch, called his student, and set off with him through the forest. Soon they reached the middle of the woods, where the teacher extinguished the torch, without explanation. "What is the matter?" asked the student. "This torch has gone out," the teacher answered and walked on. "But," shouted the student, his voice plucking his fear, "will you leave me here in the dark?" "No! I will not leave you in the dark," returned the teacher's voice from the surrounding blackness. "I will leave you searching for the light."

SOURCES

INTRODUCTION

x André Malraux, *Anti-memoirs,* trans. Terence Kilmartin (New York: Holt, Rinehart, and Winston, 1968), p. 1.

x M. Scott Peck, *The Road Less Traveled: A New Psychology of Love, Traditional Values and Spiritual Growth* (New York: Touchstone, 1978), p. 97.

THE WAY OF SOUL IS LOVE

THE LOVE OF OTHERS

5 Thomas Moore, *Care of the Soul* (New York: Harper Perennial, 1992), p. 73.

6 Jalālu'l-Dīn Rūmi, in *The Essential Rumi,* trans. Coleman Barks (New York: HarperCollins, 1995), p. 243.

7 Desiderius Erasmus, *The Praise of Folly,* trans. Betty Radice (London: Penguin Books, 1971), p. 35.

8 Confucius, *Analects,* trans. D. C. Lau (London: Penguin Books, 1979), Book XIII, saying 24, p. 122.

8 Noah benShea, *The Word: Jewish Wisdom through Time* (New York: Villard Books, 1995), p. 92.

9 Lao Tzu, *Tao Te Ching,* trans. Raymond Bernard Blakney (New York: Knopf, 1955), p. 54.

10 Marianne Williamson, *A Return to Love: Reflections on the Principles of a Course in Miracles* (New York: Harper Perennial, 1993), p. 136.

11 Plato, *On Homosexuality: Lysis, Phaedrus, and Symposium,* trans.

Benjamin Jowett (New York: Prometheus Books, 1991), pp. 121–125.

12 *Kabbala: The True Science of Light* (Philadelphia: J. M. Stoddart, 1877).

13 Kuan Tao-Sheng, "Married Love," in *Women Poets of China,* trans. Kenneth Rexroth and Ling Chung (New York: New Directions, 1990), p. 53.

14 Eviatar Zerubavel, *The Fine Line: Making Distinctions in Everyday Life* (New York: Free Press, 1991), p. 86.

16 Leonard Cohen, "Anthem," in *Stranger Music: Selected Poems and Songs* (New York: Vintage Books, 1994), p. 374.

16 Sufi tale, in Rick Fields with Peggy Taylor, Rex Wyler, and Rick Ingrasci, *Chop Wood, Carry Water* (New York: Putnam, 1984).

18 Thomas Aquinas, in Frederic Brussat and Mary Ann Brussat, *Spiritual Literacy: Reading the Sacred in Everyday Life* (New York: Touchstone, 1996), p. 177.

18 Course in Miracles prayer, in Williamson, *Return to Love,* p. 17.

19 Rainer Maria Rilke, *Letters to a Young Poet,* trans. M. D. Herter Norton (New York: Norton, 1993), Letter seven, Rome, May 14, 1904, pp. 52–60.

20 Thomas A. Harris, *I'm OK, You're OK* (New York: Avon Books, 1969), pp. 69–71.

21 *God's Word,* Genesis 3:11–13, (Grand Rapids, Mich.: World Publishing, 1995), p. 3.

22 Robertson Davies, *Fifth Business* (Toronto: Macmillan of Canada, 1970), p. 259.

24 Henrik Ibsen, *Four Great Plays by Henrik Ibsen,* trans. R. Farquharson Sharp (New York: Bantam Books, 1981), pp. 293–294.

26 Kalman Glantz and John K. Pearce, *Exiles from Eden: Psychotherapy from an Evolutionary Perspective* (New York: Norton, 1989), p. 133.

28 Francis William Bourdillon, in Kenneth J. Gergen, *The Saturated Self: Dilemmas of Identity in Contemporary Life* (New York: Basic Books, 1991), p. 20.

29 Norman Cousins, in Brussat and Brussat, *Spiritual Literacy,* p. 154.

29 *Bhagavad Gita,* trans. Angirasa Muni (Fort Wayne, Ind: Sacred Books, 1999), Vol. III, pp. 185, 347.

30 Martin Luther King, Jr., in Brussat and Brussat, *Spiritual Literacy,* p. 154.

30 David W. Ausburger, ibid., p. 155.

30 M. Scott Peck, *Further Along the Road Less Traveled: The Unending Journey Toward Spiritual Growth* (New York: Touchstone, 1993), p. 159.

31 Solomon Islands, in Robert Fulghum, *All I Need to Know I Learned in Kindergarten: Uncommon Thoughts on Common Things* (New York: Ballantine Books, 1988), p. 17.

31 Frederick Buechner, *Wishful Thinking: A Seeker's ABC* (San Francisco: Harper SanFrancisco, 1993), p. 2.

32 *God's Word,* Matthew 26:31–35, p. 1249.

33 Thomas Moore, *Soul Mates* (New York: Harper Perennial, 1994), p. 68.

33 Montaigne, in Marion F. Solomon, *Lean on Me: The Power of Positive Dependency in Intimate Relationships* (New York: Simon & Schuster, 1994), p. 46.

33 Ibid.

34 Sufi parable, "The ancient coffer of Nuri Bey," in Moore, *Care of the Soul,* p. 124.

35 Ambrose Bierce, *The Devil's Dictionary* (New York: Castle Books, 1967), p. 17.

36 Amotz Zahavi, "The testing of a bond," *Animal Behavior* 25 (1976): 246–247.

37 Sky maiden, in Harold Kushner, *Who Needs God* (New York: Pocket Books, 1991), pp. 11–12.

37 *The Complete Poems of Emily Dickinson,* ed. Thomas H. Johnson (Boston: Little, Brown, 1960), verse 303, p. 143.

38 Walter W. Benjamin, *Illuminations: Essays and Reflections* (New York: Schocken Books, 1968), pp. 168–169.

38 Friedrich Nietzsche, *Beyond Good and Evil: Prelude to a Philosophy of the Future,* trans. Walter Kaufmann (New York: Vintage Books, 1966), p. 92.

38 John O'Donohue, *Eternal Echoes: Exploring Our Yearning to Belong* (New York: Cliff Street Books, 1999), p. xxi.

THE LOVE OF WORK

41 O'Donohue, *Eternal Echoes,* p. 153.

42 Marsilio Ficino, *Marcilio Ficino: The Book of Life,* trans. Charles Boer (Dallas: Spring Publications, 1980), p. 17.

43 Sigmund Freud, in Erik Erikson, *Identity and the Life Cycle* (New York: International Universities Press, 1968), p. 96.

43 St. Thérèse, in Brussat and Brussat, *Spiritual Literacy,* p. 236.

44 Marceau, in Otto Kernberg, *Severe Personality Disorder* (New Haven: Yale University Press, 1984), p. 196.

44 Willigis Jager, *Search for the Meaning of Life: Essays and Reflections on the Mystical Experience* (Liguori, Mo.: Triumph Books, 1995), p. 115.

45 Aryeh Kaplan, *Jewish Meditation* (New York: Pantheon Books, 1985), p. 143.

45 Mary McDermott Shideler, *Spirituality: An Approach Through Descriptive Psychology* (Ann Arbor, Mich.: Descriptive Psychology Press, 1992), p. 80.

46 Suzuki Roshi, in Bettina Vitell, *Taste of Heaven and Earth* (New York: HarperCollins, 1993), p. 119.

47 Wendell Johnson, *People in Quandaries* (New York: Harper & Row, 1989), p. 278.

48 Bertrand Russell, letter from prison to Constance Malleson, 1918, in *The Selected Letters of Bertrand Russell,* ed. Nicholas Griffin (Boston: Houghton Mifflin, 1992).

50 Paul Nystrom, *Economics of Fashion* (New York: Ronald Press, 1928), pp. 68–69.

51 Gary Zukav, *The Seat of the Soul* (New York: Fireside, 1990), p. 150.

51 Suny Buffalo experiment (unpublished). Jennifer Crocker and Lisa Gallo "The Self-enhancing Effect of Downward Comparison." Paper presented at the American Psychological Association Convention, August 1985.

52 Henri Bergson, *Creative Evolution,* trans. Arthur Mitchell (London: Macmillan, 1911), p. ix.

52 John of the Cross, in O'Donohue, *Eternal Echoes,* p. 79.

53 Letty Cottin Pogrebin, in Brussat and Brussat, *Spiritual Literacy,* p. 420.

54 Jalālu'l-Dīn Rūmi, in *Essential Rumi,* p. 1.

55 Donna Schaper, *Stripping Down* (San Diego: LuraMedia, 1991), p. 7.

56 René Descartes, *Discourse on Method and Related Writings,* trans. Desmond M. Clarke (New York: Penguin Books, 1999), pp. 70–71.

56 James Hillman, *The Myth of Analysis* (New York: Harper Perennial, 1992), p. 92.

57 Nicholas of Cusa, in Moore, *Care of the Soul,* p. 290.

58 Nasreddin, ibid., pp. 122–123.

58 Shunryu Suzuki, *Zen Mind, Beginner's Mind* (New York: Weatherhill, 1998), p. 63.

58 Marge Piercy, "To Be of Use," in *Circles on the Water* (New York: Knopf, 2000), p. 106.

59 Gershom Scholem, *On the Kabbalah and Its Symbolism* (New York: Schocken Books, 1965), pp. 111–112.

60 Moore, *Care of the Soul,* p. 187.

60 Jean Renoir, in Solomon, *Lean on Me,* p. 117.

61 Akenfield village in Ronald Blythe, *Akenfield: Portrait of an English Village* (New York, Pantheon Books, 1969), p. 54.

62 Robert Burton, *The Anatomy of Melancholy* (1621), ed. Holbrook Jackson (New York: New York Review Books, 2001), p. 20.

62 David Seabury, *The Art of Selfishness* (New York: Cornerstone Library, 1973), p. 180.

63 David J. Wolpe, *Teaching Your Children About God* (New York: Holt, 1993), p. 214.

64 Moses, *God's Word,* Numbers 11:11–15, p. 168.

65 William James, "But if you treat life abstractly," in Charles Pelham Curtis and Ferris Greenslet, *The Practical Cogitator or The Thinker's Anthology* (New York: Dell, 1975), p. 60.

66 Antonio Machado, in *Times Alone: Selected Poems of Antonio Machado,* trans. Robert Bly (Middletown, Conn.: Wesleyan University Press, 1983), p. 43.

The Love of Belonging

67 James Hillman, *The Soul's Code: In Search of Character and Calling* (New York: Warner Books, 1997), p. 41.

71 *God's Word,* Genesis 2:7, p. 2.

75 Robert S. Weiss, "Attachment in Adult Life," in Colin Murray Parkes and Joan Stevenson-Hinde, eds., *The Place of Attachment in Human Behavior* (New York: Basic Books, 1982), p. 174.

75 Peter L. Berger, *A Far Glory: A Quest for Faith in an Age of Credulity* (New York: Free Press, 1992), pp. 87–90.

76 Erich Fromm, *Escape from Freedom* (New York: Henry Holt, 1969), pp. 28–30, 32.

76 Robert A. Nisbet, *The Quest for Community: A Study in the Ethics of Order and Freedom* (New York: Oxford University Press, 1953), p. 230.

77 King David in God's Word, 2 Samuel 1:25, p. 354.

79 Williamson, *Return to Love,* p. 115.

80 Kenneth Gergen, *Saturated Self: Dilemmas of Identity in Contemporary Life* (New York: Basic Books, 1991), pp. 210–224.

82 Rabbi story, in Harold Kushner, *When Bad Things Happen to Good People* (New York: Avon Books, 1981), p. 110.

82 Chinese tale, ibid., pp. 110–111.

83 Hagao Kawai, *Buddhism and the Art of Psychotherapy* (College Station: Texas A&M University Press, 1996), p. 4.

84 Zen saying, in Brussat and Brussat, *Spiritual Literacy,* p. 353.

85 Thomas Moore, *Original Self: Living with Paradox and Authenticity* (New York: HarperCollins, 2000), p. 28.

85 Turkish tale, in Oner Yagci, *Nasreddin Hoca Ve Fikralari* (Istanbul: Engin Yayincilik, 1994), p. 169.

85 Dalai Lama and Howard Cutler, *The Art of Happiness: A Handbook for Living* (New York: Riverhead Books, 1998), p. 57.

86 Voltaire, *Candide,* Lowell Blair, trans. (New York: Bantam Books, 1981), p. 120.

87 Joseph Campbell, in Brussat and Brussat, *Spiritual Literacy,* p. 31.

89 Menon story, in Fulghum, *All I Need to Know I Learned in Kindergarten,* p. 152.

90 Mahatma Gandhi, in Wayne Muller, *Legacy of the Heart: The Spiritual Advantages of a Painful Childhood* (New York: Simon & Schuster, 1992), p. 182.

92 Joel Kovel, *History and Spirit: An Inquiry into the Philosophy of Liberation* (Boston: Beacon Press, 1991), p. 221.

92 Abraham Lincoln, in James Redfield, *The Celestine Vision: Living the New Spiritual Awareness* (New York: Warner Books, 1997), p. 14.

93 Harold Kushner, *Who Needs God,* p. 204.

93 Teresa of Avila, in Brussat and Brussat, *Spiritual Literacy,* p. 325.

95 G. K. Chesterton, *Heretics* (New York: John Lane, 1905), p. 97.

96 Henry David Thoreau, *Walden and Other Writings* (New York: Barnes & Noble Books, 1993), p. 267.

96 Moore, *Care of the Soul,* p. 227.

98 William Barrett, *Irrational Man* (New York: Doubleday, 1962), p. 35.

98 Robert M. Pirsig, *Zen and the Art of Motorcycle Maintenance* (New York: Bantam Books, 1989), p. 190.

99 Kushner, *When Bad Things Happen,* pp. 121–122.

99 Harry Golden, ibid., p. 121.

100 Emile Durkheim, *The Elementary Forms of the Religious Life* (London: Allen & Unwin, 1915), pp. 59, 466.

100 Berger, *Far Glory,* p. 81.

THE WAY OF SPIRIT IS BELIEVING

103 Hillman, *Soul's Code,* p. 10.

BELIEVING IN THE SACRED

105 Mechtild of Magdeburg, in Brussat and Brussat, *Spiritual Literacy,* p. 167.

108 Joseph Campbell, *The Hero with a Thousand Faces* (New York: Pantheon Books, 1949), p. 322.

109 Paul Tillich, *The Shaking of the Foundations* (New York: Charles Scribner's Sons, 1948), p. 159.

111 Yūnus Emre, in *The Poetry of Yūnus Emre, a Turkish Sufi Poet,* ed. and trans. Grace Martin Smith (Los Angeles: University of California Press, 1993), p. 101.

112 Hillman, *Soul's Code,* p. 35.

113 Jacob, in Burton L. Visotsky, *The Genesis of Ethics* (New York: Three Rivers Press, 1996), p. 187.

113 William Shakespeare, *Macbeth,* in *Shakespearean Tragedies* (London: Collins, 1937), p. 121.

117 Rudyard Kipling, in Robert J. Ringer, *Looking Out for Number 1* (New York: Fawcett Crest, 1977), p. 171.

118 William Blake, in Williamson, *Return to Love,* p. 32.

120 Jean-Paul Sartre, personal communication.

122 Viktor E. Frankl, *Man's Search for Meaning: An Introduction to Logotherapy* (New York: Pocket Books, 1959) p. 105.

123 Zukav, *Seat of the Soul,* p. 195.

123 O'Donohue, *Eternal Echoes,* pp. 166–168.

123 Plato, *The Republic,* trans. Benjamin Jowett (New York: Barnes & Noble, 1991), Book VII, pp. 209–212.

124 Robert Bly, *Iron John: A Book About Men* (New York: Vintage Books, 1992), p. 209.

128 Berrien Berands, in Brussat and Brussat, *Spiritual Literacy,* p. 432.

129 Zen story, in Sogyal Rinpoche, *The Tibetan Book of Living and Dying* (San Francisco: HarperSanFrancisco, 1994), p. 79

129 Ibid., pp. 53–54.

130 Jalālu'l-Dīn Rūmi, "The relativity of evil," in *Rumi: Poet and Mystic,* ed. and trans. Reynold A. Nicholson (Oxford: Oneworld, 1995), p. 152.

130 Paracelsus, *Selected Writings,* ed. Jolande Jacobi, trans. Norbert Guterman (Princeton: Princeton University Press, 1979), p. 49.

130 Song variation, in Timothy Miller, *How to Want What You Have: Discovering the Magic and Grandeur of Ordinary Existence* (New York: Henry Holt, 1995), pp. 163–164.

131 Ibid.

132 Tom Harpur, *The Uncommon Touch: An Investigation of Spiritual Healing* (Toronto: McClelland & Stewart, 1994), pp. 61–62.

132 Herbert Benson, *Timeless Healing: The Power and Biology of Belief* (New York: Simon & Schuster, 1977), p. 161.

BELIEVING IN UNITY

133 Matthew W. Fox, *The Coming of the Cosmic Christ* (San Francisco: HarperCollins, 1988), p. 32.

134 "The Black Book of Carmarthan," in Robert van de Weyer, *Celtic Fire* (New York: Doubleday, 1990), pp. 170–171.

134 Jalālu'l-Dīn Rūmi, "Say I Am You," in *Essential Rumi,* pp. 275–276.

138 Ralph Waldo Emerson, "Self-Reliance," in *The Portable Emerson,* ed. Carl Bode and Malcolm Cowley (New York: Penguin, 1981), p. 149.

138 Robert Sardello, *Facing the World with Soul* (New York: Harper Perennial, 1994), pp. 49–51.

139 Randolph M. Nesse and George C. Williams, *Why We Get Sick* (New York: Random House, 1995), p. 249.

140 John Wheeler in Deepak Chopra, *Ageless Body, Timeless Mind* (New York: Harmony Books, 1993), p. 283.

140 Ernst Bloch, in O'Donohue, *Eternal Echoes,* p. 119.

146 Joseph Campbell with Bill Moyers, *The Power of Myth* (New York: Doubleday, 1988), p. 22.

147 Wendell Berry, *Sex, Economy, Freedom and Community: Eight Essays* (New York: Pantheon Books, 1994), p. 103.

147 Brussat and Brussat, *Spiritual Literacy,* pp. 527–528.

148 Scott Russell Sanders, *Staying Put* (Boston: Beacon Press, 1993), pp. 120–121.

148 Buddha, in Brussat and Brussat, *Spiritual Literacy,* p. 121.

149 O'Donohue, *Eternal Echoes,* pp. 176–178.

149 Odysseus, in Campbell, *Power of Myth,* p. 134.

150 Anthony Storr, *Solitude: A Return to the Self* (New York: Ballantine Books, 1989), p. 36.

151 Thoreau, *Walden,* p. 107.

151 Storr, *Solitude,* p. 188.

153 Leonard Shengold, *Soul Murder: The Effects of Childhood Abuse and Deprivation* (New Haven: Yale University Press, 1989).

154 Franz Kafka, in *The Blue Octavo Notebooks,* ed. Max Brod, trans. Ernst Kaiser and Eithne Wilkins (Cambridge, Mass.: Exact Change, 1991), p. 98.

154 Jalālu'l-Dīn Rūmi, in *Rumi: Poet and Mystic,* p. 51.

155 Moses, in Kushner, *When Bad Things Happen,* p. 135.

156 Campbell, *Power of Myth,* p. xvi.

157 John R. Howe, in Sean O'Reilly, James O'Reilly, and Tim O'Reilly, eds., *The Road Within: True Stories of Transformation* (San Francisco: O'Reilly, 1997), p. 44.

157 Peck, *Road Less Traveled,* p. 95.

158 Michael Talbot, *The Holographic Universe* (New York: Harper Perennial, 1991), p. 41.

BELIEVING IN TRANSFORMATION

163 O'Donohue, *Eternal Echoes,* p. 166.

163 W. H. Auden, "The Dark Years," in *Collected Poems* (New York: Random House, 1976), p. 223.

164 Sogyal Rinpoche, *Tibetan Book of Living and Dying,* p. 116.

164 Old Irish ballad, in Nesse and Williams, *Why We Get Sick,* p. 107.

165 Sogyal Rinpoche, *Tibetan Book of Living and Dying,* p. 250.

166 Elisabeth Kübler-Ross, *On Death and Dying* (New York: Macmillan, 1969), pp. 34–43, 44–71, 72–74, 98, 99–121.

167 Robert Fulghum, *From Beginning to End* (New York: Villard Books, 1995), p. 400.

168 W. Somerset Maugham, *A Traveller in Romance: Uncollected Writings, 1961–1964,* ed. John Whitehead (New York: Potter, 1984).

169 Kathleen Raine, *Collected Poems* (New York: Random House, 1956), p. 83.

170 Fyodor Dostoevski, *The Idiot,* trans. Henry and Olga Carlisle (New York: New American Library, 1969), pp. 61–62.

171 The Koran (Qur'an), in Jalalu'l Dīn Rūmi, *The Essential Rumi,* p. 1.

172 Jean-François Revel and Matthieu Ricard, *The Monk and the Philosopher* (New York: Schocken Books, 1998), p. 282.

173 Albert Camus, "Summer in Algiers," in *The Myth of Sisyphus and Other Essays* (New York: Vintage Books, 1991), p. 153.

173 *God's Word,* Ecclesiastes 9:11, p. 836.

174 Percy Bysshe Shelley, "Ozymandias," in *The Complete Poems of Percy Bysshe Shelley* (New York: Modern Library, 1994), p. 589.

176 William Blake, "Auguries of Innocence," in *Blake: Complete Writings* (New York: Oxford University Press, 1972), p. 431.

177 Ananda K. Coomaraswamy, "Akimkanna: Self-Naughting" *The New Indian Antiquary,* vol. 3 (Bombay: n.p., 1940), p. 6.

177 Revel and Ricard, *Monk and the Philosopher,* p. 88.

177 Sogyal Rinpoche, *Tibetan Book of Living and Dying,* p. 37.

178 Revel and Ricard, *Monk and the Philosopher,* p. 278.

179 Friedrich Nietzsche, *Thus Spoke Zarathustra,* trans. Walter Kaufmann (New York: Penguin Books, 1978), pp.158, 217, 220–221.

179 *The Upanishads,* trans. Eknath Easwaran (Tomales, Calif: Nilgiri Press, 1987), p. 149.

180 Chopra, *Seven Spiritual Laws of Success,* p. 111.

181 *God's Word,* Ecclesiastes 2:4–11, p. 828.

182 *The Tibetan Book of the Dead,* trans. Robert A. F. Thurman (New York: Bantam Books, 1994), p. 20.

184 M. C. Richards, *Centering in Pottery, Poetry, and the Person* (Middletown, Conn.: Wesleyan University Press, 1989), p. 13.

186 Sufi tale, in A. R. Arastah and A. A. Sheikh, "Sufism: The Way to Universal Self," in A. A. Sheikh and K. S. Sheikh, *Healing East and West: Ancient Wisdom and Modern Psychology* (New York: Wiley, 1989), p. 159.

187 Zukav, *Seat of the Soul,* pp. 185–186.

187 Hillman, *Soul's Code,* p. 46.

187 *The Aeneid of Virgil,* trans. Alan Mandelbaum (New York: Bantam Books, 1981), Book VI, verses 988–993, p. 157.

THE WAY OF GOD IS BELIEVING AND LOVING

SECULAR APOSTLE

191 Kushner, *Who Needs God,* pp. 138–139.

BELIEVING IN GOD

193 Chopra, *How to Know God.*

195 Karl Jaspers, *Way to Wisdom: An Introduction to Philosophy* (New Haven: Yale University Press, 1954), p. 48.

195 Karen Armstrong, *A History of God: The 4,000-Year Quest of Judaism, Christianity, and Islam* (New York: Knopf, 1993), p. xx.

196 Giovanni Pico della Mirandola, "Instruction from God," in *The Renaissance Philosophy of Man,* eds. Ernst Cassirer, Paul Oskar Kristeller, and John H. Randall, Jr. (Chicago: University of Chicago Press, 1948), p. 225.

196 Gabriel García Márquez, *One Hundred Years of Solitude,* trans. Gregory Rabassa (Franklin Center, Pa.: Franklin Library, 1981), p. 187.

197 Ana-Maria Rizzuto, *The Birth of the Living God: A Psychoanalytic Study* (Chicago: University of Chicago Press, 1979), p. 52.

198 Armstrong, *History of God,* p. 376.

198 Paul Tillich, "Religion," in *Man's Right to Knowledge* (New York: Columbia University Press, 1954), pp. 79–80.

199 Lynne Cox, "To Aqaba," in O'Reilly, O'Reilly, and Reilly, *Road Within,* p. 84.

BELIEVING IN THE EXISTENCE OF GOD IN THE FORM OF ABSENCE

201 Jalālu'l-Dīn Rūmi, in *Essential Rumi,* p. 136.

201 Gospel of Thomas, in R. A. Mayotte, *The Complete Jesus* (South Royalton, Vt.: Steerforth Press, 1997), p. 74.

202 benShea, *The Word,* p. 30.

203 Tertullian, "*De carne Christi* (On the Flesh of Christ)," in *Tertullian's Treatise on the Incarnation,* ed. and trans. Ernest Evans (London: SPCK, 1956), ch. 5, p. 4.

204 Simone Weil, in O'Donohue, *Eternal Echoes,* p. 268.

204 G. K. Chesterton, in Shideler, *Spirituality,* p. 2.

204 Colin Wilson, *Poetry and Mysticism* (San Francisco: City Lights, 1969), pp. 14–15.

205 Chopra, *How to Know God* (New York: Harmony Books, 2000), p. 196.

205 Kushner, *Who Needs God,* p. 153.

206 Charlotte Joko Beck, *Everyday Zen: Love and Work* (San Francisco: Harper San Francisco, 1989), p. 182.

207 Louis Pasteur, in Brussat and Brussat, *Spiritual Literacy,* p. 139.

207 Suzuki, *Zen Mind, Beginner's Mind,* p. 46.

THE LOVE OF GOD

209 Beck, *Everyday Zen,* p. 5.

209 Yūnus Emre, in *Poetry of Yūnus Emre,* p. 5.

210 Moore, *Original Self,* p. 12.

210 Beck, *Everyday Zen,* p. 122.

211 Jalālu'l-Dīn Rūmi, in *Essential Rumi,* p. xi.

211 Smith, *The Poetry of Yūnus Emre,* p. 136.

211 Jalālu'l-Dīn Rūmi, in *Rumi: Poet and Mystic,* p. 184.

211 *God's Word,* Mark 8:27–29, p. 1268.

212 Gospel of Thomas, in Arno Gruen, *The Betrayal of the Self* (New York: Grove Press, 1988), p. 86.

212 Harold Schulweis, in Kushner, *Who Needs God,* p. 203.

THE LOVE OF DIVINE LAW

213 Jalālu'l-Dīn Rūmi, in *Essential Rumi,* p. 255.

213 G. Peter Fleck, in Kushner, *Who Needs God,* p. 75.

215 Peck, *Road Less Traveled,* p. 97.

216 James P. Carse, *Breakfast at the Victory* (New York: HarperCollins, 1994), p. 19.

217 God's Word, Genesis 18:20–32, p. 19.

218 Christopher Lasch, *The Culture of Narcissism: American Life in an Age of Diminishing Expectations* (New York: Norton, 1978), p. 55.

EPILOGUE: UNTYING THE ENDS, FALLIBLY

219 Anthony Hecht, "Terms," in *The Transparent Man: Poems* (New York: Knopf, 1990).

219 Dalai Lama and Cutler, *Art of Happiness,* pp. 306–307.

219 Wayne Oates, in Peck, *Further Along the Road Less Traveled,* pp. 107–108.

220 Brussat and Brussat, *Spiritual Literacy,* p. 10.

220 Martin Buber, *I and Thou,* trans. Walter Kaufmann (New York: Touchstone, 1996), pp. 25–26, 144.

220 Winifred Gallagher, *Working on God* (New York: Random House, 1999), p. 161.

221 John R. Gribbin, *The Omega Point: The Search for the Missing Mass and the Ultimate Fate of the Universe* (New York: Bantam Books, 1988), p. 22.

221 Ringer, *Looking Out for Number One,* pp. 19–20.

222 O'Donohue, *Eternal Echoes,* p. 257.

222 Chandrasekharendra Saraswati, *The Vedas* (Bombay: Bharatiya Vidya Bhavan, 1988), pp. 35–36, 65.

222 Christian Bede Griffiths, in Brussat and Brussat, *Spiritual Literacy*, p. 18.

223 Meister Eckhart, ibid.

223 Gallagher, *Working on God* p. xvi.

223 Jean Shinoda Bolen, *Crossing to Avalon* (San Francisco: Harper, 1995), p. 34.

224 St. Teresa of Avila, in P. M. H. Atwater, *Future Memory: How Those Who "See the Future" Shed New Light on the Workings of the Human Mind* (Charlottesville, Va.: Hampton Roads, 1999), pp. 176–177.

224 Sam Keen, *To a Dancing God: Notes of a Spirited Traveler* (San Francisco: Harper & Row, 1990), p. 22.

224 benShea, *The Word,* p. 311.

PERMISSIONS

ABOUT THE AUTHOR

T. BYRAM KARASU, M.D., is a renowned physician, psychiatrist, author, and lecturer. He completed his training at Yale University and is currently Silverman Professor and the University Chairman of the Department of Psychiatry and Behavioral Sciences at the Albert Einstein College of Medicine and Psychiatrist-in-Chief of Montefiore Medical Center.

Dr. Karasu's previous books were praised variously as "extraordinary," and "gold medal, perfect ten." "What a brave book!" Peter Kramer, the author of *Listening to Prozac,* says about his latest, *The Psychotherapist as Healer.* Dr. Karasu is currently editor in chief of the *American Journal of Psychotherapy* and Distinguished Life Fellow of the American Psychiatric Association. He has been the recipient of numerous awards, including the American Psychiatric Association's Presidential Commendation.

Dr. Karasu chaired the American Psychiatric Association's Commission on Psychiatric Therapies, as well as a national task force with the goal of producing a seminal document describing the treatment of each psychiatric disorder. This four-volume report, *Treatments of Psychiatric Disorder,* has been praised as "twenty-five years ahead of its time" (*Atlantic Monthly*) and "the best psychiatric book ever" (*Contemporary Psychiatry*).

Dr. Karasu also lectures extensively throughout the United States and abroad. He lives in New York City and Westport, Connecticut.